Praise for

Hearts and Minds

"Vince Parrillo and co-author Maboud Ansari present a compelling and rich qualitative, cross-cultural, and comparative examination of Gülen pedagogical philosophy, which is at the heart of Hizmet schools found around the world. The authors poignantly document how the role of teachers, the curriculum, and cultural values aligned with Islamic teachings produce change agents committed to a lifetime of service and social betterment for all. Their work is elaborately documented and rendered in a manner that drives the reader to consider how Gülen philosophy can be applied to any society seeking moral repair and advancement for all. "
~ **H. Mark Ellis**, Professor of Sociology and Criminal Justice,
  William Paterson University, United States

"After the Velvet Revolution in 1989, Vince Parrillo was a very important voice from the free world. His words, both spoken and written have made a great impact on our social thinking and continue to do so. Professor Parrillo has proved to be one of the truly sound voices of the very dramatic, if not disturbing, state of affairs in the world today – always scholarly qualified, daring and brave, as the manuscript *Hearts and Minds* again confirms."
~ **Josef Jařab**, Professor, Palacký University, Olomouc, Czechia
  University Rector Emeritus, former Czech Senator

"Vince Parrillo has been internationally known for many years as an important American voice in the field of Ethnic and Migration Studies. With this book, written with Maboud Ansari, he provides a comparative study of the Hizmet school networks in different countries. It is a valuable contribution to academic and political debates on interethnic relations and religious transnationalism."
~ **Marco Martiniello**, Research Director FRS_FNRS,
  Liège University, Belgium

"This impressive study takes the reader on an intellectual journey which focuses on showing how Hizmet schools promote dialogue and mutual respect among peoples regardless of religious background, ethnicity, and cultures. This book will prove an invaluable resource for those scholars, students, and educators, especially of comparative religion, education, and sociology who are interested in studying these topics from a cross-cultural, comparative perspective."
~ **Wieslaw Oleksy**, Professor, University of Łódź, Poland

"This book of comparative research wisely comes out with a valid and effective historiography that verifies pedagogical assumptions, didactic formulas, professional behaviors of Gülen's philosophy and the Hizmet schools, devoted to overcoming all discrimination in the name of common human belonging."
~ **Mario Aldo Toscano**, Professor, University of Pisa, Italy

"Vincent Parrillo stands out as a soundly scientific scholar who is keenly aware of moral matters. In Hearts and Minds, he and Maboud Ansari offer a skillful analysis of a schooling model, operating in many nations, which seeks to promote the same fusion of scientific skills with compassionate humanity. The authors tell an engaging story that offers important lessons for a troubled world."
~ **John J. Macionis**, Professor Emeritus, Kenyon College, USA
   Prentice Hall Distinguished Scholar

HEARTS AND MINDS

Hizmet Schools and Interethnic Relations

Vincent N. Parrillo

Maboud Ansari

BLUE DOME

Published by Blue Dome Press
335 Clifton Ave.
Clifton, NJ, 07011, USA
www.bluedomepress.com

ISBN: 978-1-68206-032-2
E-book: 978-1-68206-537-2

Library of Congress Cataloging-in-Publication Data

Names: Parrillo, Vincent N., author. | Ansari, Maboud, author.
Title: Hearts and minds : Hizmet schools and interethnic relations /
    Vincent N. Parrillo, Maboud Ansari.
Description: Clifton, NJ : Blue Dome Press, 2022. | Includes
    bibliographical references and index.
Identifiers: LCCN 2021061896 (print) | LCCN 2021061897 (ebook) | ISBN
    9781682060322 (paperback) | ISBN 9781682065372 (ebook)
Subjects: LCSH: Charter schools--Cross-cultural studies. |
    Education--Religious aspects--Islam. | Gülen Hizmet Movement. | Gülen,
    Fethullah. | Comparative education.
Classification: LCC LB2806.36 .P37 2022 (print) | LCC LB2806.36 (ebook) |
    DDC 371.05--dc23/eng/20220124
LC record available at https://lccn.loc.gov/2021061896
LC ebook record available at https://lccn.loc.gov/2021061897

Cover image by Getty Images

TABLE OF CONTENTS

About the Authors

Vincent N. Parrillo, Professor Emeritus at William Paterson University, is author of a dozen books, including *Strangers to These Shores*, 12th ed. (Pearson 2019); *Diversity in America*, 4th ed. (Routledge 2013); and *Guardians of the Gate* (iUniverse 2011). Many of his scholarly articles have been published in one of ten languages. A past Fulbright recipient and a visiting professor at the University of Liege and University of Pisa, he was also keynote speaker at a dozen international conferences in Asia, Canada, and Europe. He wrote, narrated, and co-produced six award-winning PBS documentaries. A past vice president of the Eastern Sociological Society, he was its Robin M. Williams Jr. Distinguished Lecturer in 2006.

Maboud Ansari is also a past Fulbright recipient and Professor Emeritus at William Paterson University. A graduate of Tehran University, he received advanced degrees in sociology from The University of New School in New York. He authored two books: *The Making of the Iranian Community in America* (Pardis Press 1992); *The Iranian Americans* (Edwin Mellen 2013). He is a board member of the Persian Cultural and Islamic Cultural Center.

Authors' Note

This is a book we wanted to write in 2016. However, to protect the many helpful people whom we planned to name and thank, we held back because of the purge against those associated with the Gülen movement initiated by the Turkish dictator, Recep Tayyip Erdoğan. That unwarranted action continues to date—and tens of thousands of innocent Turks have been imprisoned, ousted from their jobs, expelled or banned from traveling. According to numerous reliable sources, over 160,000 judges, teachers, medical doctors, police, and civil servants were suspended or dismissed, together with about 77,000 formally arrested.

The oppression became even more pronounced after more than 1,000 academics (including a few whom we had met) signed a petition in January 2016, protesting tank and helicopter attacks on Kurdish villages in southeast Turkey that killed hundreds and displaced thousands. Most were fired, had their passports revoked to prevent them from leaving the country. More than 500 were indicted, charged with "propagandizing for a terrorist group." Judges, following government orders, have since sentenced most of them to prison terms.

In this ongoing repression of freedom of speech and vilification of a movement, of which we are not members but respect, we have decided to go ahead with this publication that offers unbiased insights into what our field research revealed. We are keeping this book as originally intended: an objective, intellectual inquiry into the effectiveness of Gülen-inspired schools in achieving their goals even while operating in disparate socio-cultural environments.

The reader should note that we are reporting about these schools as we found them at the time of our visits. We cannot verify how these institutions are affiliated today. Because of Turkish pressures on other governments, administrations at some of these schools may have changed hands.

As we discuss our findings, we will avoid the use of names to protect those individuals and their families still living in Turkey from any possible reprisals. Although they remain anonymous here, we remember all of them for their hospitality and helpfulness, and we dedicate this book to them in grateful appreciation. With their permission to name them, we also want to thank Hüseyin Şentürk, Director of Publications at Blue Dome Press, for signing the book, and to Hakan Yeşilova, Editor at Blue Dome, for his excellent copy editing contributions and his efficiency in shepherding the book through the production process.

Vincent N. Parrillo
parrillov@wpunj.edu

Maboud Ansari
ansarim@wpunj.edu

Department of Sociology & Criminal Justice
William Paterson University
Wayne, NJ, USA

Prologue

N either of us are members of the Gülen movement (aka Hizmet), nor do we view ourselves as either apologists or publicists for the Gülen movement or its schools. Instead, as sociologists with an intellectual curiosity, we followed our discipline's scientific method of investigation and the formally approved research protocols of the Institutional Review Board (IRB) of our university. Some initial findings from the first three countries visited were presented at the 2015 annual meeting of the Eastern Sociological Society in Philadelphia. Other portions, following subsequent visits to the other four countries included in this study, were presented at research roundtables at our university. Our thanks go to colleagues who offered helpful suggestions through the various stages of this project's completion.

We conducted this qualitative research without any grants, and so practical considerations obliged us to spread out our travels over four years at the end of each academic year. Our field research took place before the escalation of Turkish government hostility against Gülenists, but this book was written after the failed coup attempt in July 2016. However, the content of this book is in no way motivated by recent events. Instead, it is a comparative and qualitative research study of an educational phenomenon that still functions throughout the world.

Like most people, the two of us knew nothing about the Gülen movement for most of our lives. One's path through life is occasionally helped along by others—a suggestion, a reference, or something else that guides you in a direction you might otherwise not have taken. While a sociology professor at William Paterson University in New Jersey, I had given numerous guest lectures at other nearby colleges and universities. Thus, on several occasions I had given presentations on diversity at Caldwell University in classes taught by Harriet Sepinwall, a Holocaust scholar. In 2010, unable to attend a dinner hosted by the Interfaith Dialogue Center (IDC) based in Hasbrouck Heights, New Jersey, she invited me to take her place, informing me that I would find it of great interest.

She was absolutely right. Several hundred people were in attendance, including clergy of all faiths, elected local and county officials, law enforcement personnel of all levels (local police chiefs, county sheriffs, FBI and U.S. Customs officials), other college educators, and many members of the local Turkish community. I would learn that this nonprofit organization, now known as the Peace Islands Institute, is dedicated to promoting dialogue based on mutual respect and collaboration among all peoples regardless of cultural, ethnic, or religious backgrounds. Through forums known as "Abrahamic Gatherings" led by a three-member panel of clergy representing Christianity, Judaism, and Islam, it offers a monthly series of participatory interfaith dialogues. To promote pluralism among youth, it sponsors an annual Art and Essay Contest, which draws entries from about 200 public, private, and charter schools. Another widely attended event is its annual Appreciation Dinner, which honors those in public safety or civic leadership roles.

At this first instance of my introduction to one dimension of the Hizmet movement, that term was not yet publicly used, nor was the name of Fethullah Gülen, the retired Turkish preacher and scholar who had inspired so many followers. I did learn, however, that this group sponsored cultural trips to Turkey, as several after-dinner speakers briefly mentioned their journeys and the friendships formed. Before the dinner someone connected to the organization learned of my background, and after all others had spoken, I was unexpectedly called upon to give my impressions. Taken aback, I first said that, unlike all other speakers before me, I had not been to Turkey nor did I have any friends in the room, before offering my thoughts about the diversity and warmth of friendship so evident in the room. Upon returning to my table, I was quickly assured that not only would I make new friends that night (I did), but that I would be going to Turkey (I did, on one of their cultural exchanges trips).

In addition to that incredibly memorable trip a year later, my intellectual journey advanced by reading the literature (notably *The Gülen Movement: A Sociological Analysis of a Civic Movement Rooted in Moderate Islam*, by Helen Rose Ebaugh, Springer 2010, and David Tittensor's excellent article, "The Gülen Movement and the Case of a Secret Agenda: Putting the Debate in Perspective." *Islam and Christian-Muslim Relations* 23:2 (March 2012): 163-179.

Through numerous conversations, particularly with the IDC Director who subsequently was the leader of my trip to Turkey, much of my initial curiosity was both satisfied and whetted to learn even more.

I informed Maboud Ansari, a sociology professor of comparative religion, about my experiences. Like me, he was intrigued and began to look into this movement. Upon his return from an academic conference in Chicago, at which he heard several paper presentations on the Gülen-inspired schools in particular locales (the term *Hizmet* still not used), he suggested that we do our own study from a cross-cultural perspective to determine how these schools are similar or dissimilar in those settings. That's how this project began, and it would not have been possible without him. This research was a joint undertaking and includes findings based on our interviews.

In designing our cross-cultural study, we opted to choose countries that had varied histories and ethnic compositions. We opted for some fairly homogeneous countries, some with a Muslim-majority population and others with a Muslim-minority population, as well as other countries with longstanding multicultural and multiracial societies. In choosing countries, however, our selections were constrained by limited personal funds, our free time, and personal obligations, which necessitated organization of our field research in travel segments. We would go on four annual trips to one or two countries at the end of our academic years in 2012 through 2015, but before academic years ended in each of those foreign countries.

How to make it happen though? Our starting point was the aforementioned IDC Director. Our timing was rather opportune, because those in the Hizmet movement were becoming more open publicly and so welcomed publicity. Consequently, scholars like ourselves, wanting to examine objectively their educational enterprise, were looked upon favorably. However, this decentralized movement has no directory, no national structure, let alone an international one. Those inspired by the teachings of Gülen in one region work independently of others in a different region.

So, after we considered various destinations and settled on Albania and Bosnia, it fell to the Director to gain advance clearance for us in those countries. Exploring institutional websites, he gained contact information to make inquiries. As the head of the local Hizmet organization in New Jersey, he had credibility with those abroad also in the movement, even though none knew each other. Thus, he was able to secure the assistance of facilitators in Albania and Bosnia, and they would prove to be of immense value in helping us gain access everywhere.

To ensure the smoothness of our investigative travels, the Director made arrangements for a Turkish professor of communications at Rutgers University, to accompany us. He served as our translator in securing ground transport abroad, acting as liaison to the Turkish educators we would meet, and arranging the specifics of our school visits. We sometimes had to assure reluctant school administrators that we had no intention of conducting performance evaluations akin to accreditation visits, but rather sought to learn about their schools from a comparative perspective. Further, we pledged that the identities of all respondents would remain anonymous. Once their initial concerns were overcome, we found everyone to be extremely hospitable and cooperative. And, it is critically important to state, that absolutely no one—on this first trip or the subsequent ones to other countries—put any restrictions on our selection process to find respondents. We had complete freedom to choose whom we wished to interview.

In the following years, we had other guides and/or facilitators to subsequent countries: Kazakhstan, Romania, Poland, Canada, and the United States, in that order. Each also was indispensable in making our research a reality, and we cannot express enough how appreciative we are for their wonderful help and companionship on these journeys.

I could not help thinking, both on those trips and now, about the open acceptance that those strangers accorded to us in these different countries. With their strong belief in positive group interrelations and acceptance of strangers, these Muslims truly live the universal teachings in the *Quran* (4:37) and *Bible* (Deuteronomy 10:19; Leviticus 19:34) that people of all faiths should follow. I also thought of other minority group members instantly bonding with unknown-but-like others, such as the Christians in the days of the Roman Empire drawing the symbol of a fish in the dirt as a means of secretly bonding; the Jews—whether religious or not—sharing that sense of centuries-old peoplehood; or American blacks feeling an affinity for one another simply through visual awareness. Minorities often feel an instant connection, a shared sense of identity, finding psychological nearness despite a lack of personal familiarity.

With wonderfully helpful yet unobtrusive assistance, our investigations between 2012 and 2015 in those research destinations enabled us to gain important firsthand information through observation and structured inquiry. Those findings and an analysis of them are the substance of this book.

~ Vincent N. Parrillo

1

INTRODUCTION

A great body of research exists on the life of the Turkish preacher Fethullah Gülen (1938-) as well as on the ideology, philosophy, organization, financing, motivation, and practices of the movement inspired by his teachings. Those practices include a vast network of Gülen-inspired schools, hospitals, media outlets, local and regional groups. In-depth discussions of these focal points may be found among those writings, some of them referenced at the end of this chapter.

Approaches range from holistic diagnoses of the entire movement to others examining just one aspect of this vast transnational network, or offering a detailed case study of Hizmet schools in a particular country. Tones vary from objective to positive to highly critical, one even labeling the movement as a "parapolitical organization dedicated to the pursuit of power" (e.g., Watmough and Öztürk 2018). A few publications were written by insiders, those who are part of the movement (e.g., Çetin 2007; Koç 2016). Others are by "outsider" academics (e.g., Agai 2002, Ebaugh 2010; Tittensor 2014; Turam 2007).

This research is also an outsider study with a focus on the implementation of a Gülen-inspired educational model in Europe, Central Asia, and North America. Although this field research necessitated the cooperation of those in the movement to initiate contacts, and of school officials to permit interviews, there was no cooptation in structuring the research, nor any collaboration in selecting interviewees or which countries to visit, nor any influence on what was written. This book is somewhat different from other studies in that, through in-person, semi-structured interviews, it examines and cross-culturally compares Hizmet schools from the multiple perspectives of students, alumni, parents, educators, and financial supporters in seven culturally distinct countries. Parts of this book are an expanded version of a presentation given to the Eastern Sociological Society at its annual meeting in Philadelphia in 2015.

This field research occurred over several years. We first went to Hizmet schools in three Muslim-majority countries: Bosnia-Herzegovina; Albania, and Kazakhstan, followed by on-site studies at schools in two Christian-majority countries, each with mostly homogeneous populations: Romania and Poland. To complete our cross-cultural comparisons, we next went to Hizmet schools in two Christian-majority but secular and multicultural countries: Canada and the United States.

When we began our field studies in 2012, few people outside of Turkey were cognizant of an imam known as Fethullah Gülen or anything about his followers, much less the schools they established around the world. Back in 1998, Gülen had met with other prominent religious leaders—Pope John Paul II and Chief Rabbi of Israel Eliyahu Bakshi-Doron—to discuss interfaith dialogue, but such meetings did not resonate in the public consciousness. In 2008, however, readers of *Foreign Policy and Prospect* magazine "by a landslide" voted him as "the world's top public intellectual. Then, in 2013, *Time* magazine named him as one of the world's 100 most influential people.

After the failed coup attempt in Turkey in July 2016, public awareness increased far more significantly because President Recep Tayyip Erdoğan, accused Gülen and his followers as the ones responsible. Those in the Gülen leadership, however, believe Erdoğan staged the coup himself to consolidate power and persecute those seen as opponents. Sadly, tens of thousands of Gülen followers have since been "subject to wrongful imprisonment, denial of job opportunities, cutting of health benefits, freezing of assets, and confiscation of passports," hundreds more everyday as recently as the latter half of 2020 (Judd and Holtmeier 2020).

Whatever information foreigners and researchers have about Gülen and his supporters, the existence and ultimate purpose of the Gülen-inspired schools/institutions is still unclear for some people. In all likelihood, the Turkish government's persistent accusations and its determined struggle to purge the system of everyone and everything associated with Gülen play a key role in the formation of their perception

(Luttwak 2016). Of particular interest to this study is the Gülen movement placing heavy emphasis on education, much like the Jesuit religious order in Catholicism, although there are limits to that parallel. It is the intent of this book, first, to provide insights into the mission and practices of the Hizmet schools in the seven aforementioned countries. Second to be examined is the impact of the dominant culture in each country upon what are intended as universal goals and practices.

Gülen's Philosophy of Education

According to Fethullah Gülen, education is not only a core value of the Hizmet movement, but also the main factor in a lifetime process of societal development. The happiness of a nation can only be sustained if new generations are raised with an integrity of both heart and mind. His main argument is that the supposed conflict between religious knowledge and science is a false conception. Instead, he formulates his educational philosophy by emphasizing certain passages from the *Quran* and the *Hadith* (the recorded words, actions, and the silent approval of the Islamic prophet Muhammad). He reminds his followers that the *Quran* urges mankind to think, ponder, reflect and acquire knowledge that would bring them closer to God and his creation. Moreover, the Prophet Muhammad commanded the seeking of knowledge by all Muslims as far they could research. Gülen further argues that we live in a global village and that education is the best way to serve humanity and to establish a dialogue with other civilizations (Agai 2002, Eldridge 2007).

The bedrock of all these schools, regardless of their locale, is this educational philosophy of Fethullah Gülen. He believes that schools are a "vital part of the making of human beings," and urges his followers to build new schools instead of new mosques:

> A school may be considered as a laboratory in which an elixir is offered which can prevent or heal the ills of life and teachers are the masters by whose skills and wisdom the elixir is prepared and administered (Gülen 2006).

Gülen regards this "laboratory" as more than a place for the acquisition of knowledge and skills; it is the incubation locale for developing lasting ethical values:

...[A]lthough it seems to occupy one phase of life, actually the school dominates all times and events. Every pupil re-enacts during the rest of life what he or she has learnt at school and derives continuous influence therefrom. What is learned or acquired at school may either be imagination and aspirations or specific skills and realities. But what is of importance here is that everything acquired must in some mysterious way be the key to closed doors and a guidance to the ways to virtue (Gülen 2006).

In *Toward a Global Civilization of Love and Tolerance* (2010), Gülen emphasized that education should be a blend of humanities, science, and ethical values to produce individuals who respect human rights and social justice:

A community's survival depends on idealism and good morals, as well as on being able to reach the necessary level in scientific and technological progress. For this reason, trades and crafts should be taught, beginning at least at the elementary level. A good school is not a building where only theoretical information is given, but an institution or a laboratory where students are prepared for life (Gülen 2010).

Universal, quality education that combines the "secular sciences" and humanistic values, he maintains, will bring about a new, enlightened "Golden Generation" with a better understanding and tolerance equipped with positive attitudes toward the rights of others. Gülen envisions this golden generation leading personal and community lives that would showcase Islam and encourage others to follow. Moreover, it would be a generation well-educated in science and well-rounded in moral training (Gülen 1996). "The prototype of the golden generation is the teacher of the movement who works to bring on a 'Golden Age'" (Agai 2003).

The golden generation would thus have the defining characteristics of faith and strong ethical values as the driving forces in applying science for the benefit of humankind. As Gülen puts it, "The golden generation will participate in modernity and help to shape it (Yildirim 2004). Gülen's ideal is *zul-cenaheyn*, one who possesses two wings (exhibiting a marriage of mind and heart). Consolidation of different educational currents should result in a holistic system that trains individuals in "thought, action and inspiration" to cope with the changing demands of the world. These individuals then, would use their knowledge and training for the service of humankind.

> He sees education as requisite for social, economic and political modernization and advocates that individuals will respect democratic law and human rights only if they receive a sound education. Social justice and peace, he argues, are achieved by intellectually enlightened people with strong moral values and a sense of altruism. . . This philosophy is the basis of the educational system in all the schools, primary, secondary and university level, that are inspired by Mr. Gülen's ideals (Ebaugh 2010:34).

According to Gülen, an integral component of this educational process—in fact, one that must function hand-in-glove to educate both mind and heart—is the exemplary character of teachers who have strong morality. "Education is different from teaching. Most people can teach, but only a very few can educate" (Gülen 2004:208). In other words, teaching is the transmission of knowledge, but educating also includes, according to Gülen, altruistic love and moral guidance (Nelson 2005:6). Teachers therefore play a key role in shaping students' character by teaching them true Islamic principles (Çelik 2017:33).

> The real teacher is one who sows the pure seed and preserves it. It is his duty to be occupied with what is good and wholesome and to lead and guide the child in his or her life and in the face of all events. As it is in the school that life, flowing outside in so many different directions, acquires a stable character and identity so too it is in the school that a child is cast in his or her true mold and attains to the mysteries of personality. Just as a wide full river gains force as it flows in a narrow channel so too the flowing of life in undirected ways is channeled into unity by means of the school. In like manner a fruit is a manifestation of unity growing out of the fruit-tree's diversity (Gülen 2006).

For Gülen, because teachers have such a lasting impact on impressionable young minds, it is essential that they not only encourage in the classroom the acquisition of modern knowledge and promote critical thinking, but also outside the classroom they should exemplify the essence of a "good person" with strong ethical values.

The mass media can communicate information to human beings but they can never teach real life. Teachers are irreplaceable in this respect. It is the teachers alone who find a way to the heart of the pupil and leave indelible imprints upon his or her mind. Teachers who reflect deeply and impart the truths will be able to provide good examples for their pupils and teach them the aims of the sciences. They will test the information they are going to pass on to their pupils through the refinement of their own minds not by such Western methods as are today thought to provide facile answers to everything (Gülen 2006).

Heavily inculcated in Gülen's philosophy of education is respect and tolerance for, as well as acceptance and dialogue among, people of all faiths. In his lectures and writings, he has often quoted Ali ibn Abi Talib (601-661), the fourth caliph after Muhammad, "Muslims are your brothers in religion, and non-Muslims are your human brothers" (Ünal and Williams 200:331).

Accordingly, Gülen has long encouraged community and business leaders to provide financial backing for such quality schools. As a result, Turkish businessmen—from large multinational companies or small local enterprises, at home or far-flung around the globe—have made donations of all sizes to create many hundreds of schools worldwide. They establish regional umbrella organizations that serve as educational trusts to ensure the financial stability and academic structure of schools within their purview.

These regional foundations are autonomous. Although aware of the existence of similar organizations elsewhere, no structural interconnection is in effect. Some cross-fertilization may occur with movement of educators from schools in one country to another but, in a real sense, these schools are Gülen-inspired, but not centrally controlled.

What Is Hizmet?

Hizmet is a Turkish word whose essential meaning is altruistic service for the common good; it is a derivation of the Arabic-Persian word *khidmat*, which means "service." At the outset of our investigation, this term was not openly promulgated among members of the Gülen movement. Instead, parents of students attending these schools typically referred to them as "the Turkish schools." About midway into our field research,

Hizmet began to be spoken more frequently and is thus the term incorporated in this book.

Hizmet is a shared goal of the followers of Fethullah Gülen, a Turkish Islamic scholar and author of more than 60 books. A believer in moderation and tolerance, he is an advocate of interfaith dialogue and, importantly, the reconciliation of religious faith with science and modern institutions, including democracy. Combined with his pro-business position, Gülen's approach has thus led some analysts to describe it as "Islamic Calvinism" (Mango 2006).

Inspired by his teachings and ideas, Gülen's followers in Turkey in the 1970s initiated the movement that bears his name. Highly influential in Turkey until mid-2016, Hizmet evolved into a ubiquitous transnational movement in the 1990s and is now active in more than 120 countries, enabling it to lay claim to being "one of the most significant social movements that arose from the Muslim world (Ergene 2008: vii). Drawn from the Turkish Diaspora and the diverse native populations of countries where the movement exists, a network of volunteers, educators, and business people provide the means by which the movement flourishes and expands (Balci and Miller 2012).

Hizmet Schools

One of the most remarkable things about the Gülen Movement is the rapid growth since the early 1990s of more than a thousand educational institutions (tutoring centers, K-12 schools, and universities) in Turkey (before the purge) and more than 1,000 other schools around the world (Hansen 2012). With the collapse of the Soviet Union in 1991, Gülen followers filled the vacuum and created a loose network of fee-paying private schools and universities in the post-communist countries, as well as elsewhere. They exist in most Muslim countries stretching from the Balkans to Africa, and from Central Asia to Indonesia. They also exist in many non-Muslim countries, including Japan and Mexico, numbering at their peak more than 1,400 schools in 170 countries (Çelik 2017:29). It is estimated that there are 100 schools in the US which are run or staffed by Hizmet-inspired individuals, foundations, or corporations. (Judd and Holtmeier 2020).

One significant aspect of these schools is that, although religious faith is the driving force for their creation, they do not teach religion, except for a general course on world religions comparable to that found in U.S. universities. However, they are not solely secular schools either. Instead, the schools emphasize universal, moral values which are already compatible with Islam – and the other faith traditions – as the common denominator among diverse ethnic, political and religious groups (Agai 2002:27).

The schools share a similar curriculum structure, with most subjects taught in English except for Turkish language courses and certain subjects relevant to the host country (such as its history), which are taught in the native language. Great emphasis is placed on math and science, which the schools encourage through medal competitions in international Olympiads among students from similar schools elsewhere.

Enrollment of students follows a similar pattern worldwide. In each country a private education foundation —one that coordinates the administering, teaching, and financing of the schools—conducts widely publicized entrance exams in numerous cities and towns. Because of rigorous academic standards for admittance, only the best and brightest become students. Of two dozen schools we visited, a common ratio was about 50 students accepted out of 1,300 examinees. It is therefore hardly surprising that these high schools rank among the most prestigious in their countries, or that their graduates gain acceptances at prominent universities worldwide.

Although the movement is rooted in the spiritual and humanistic traditions of Islam, critics of the Hizmet schools claim that the agenda of those running them extends beyond education to objectives of gaining power and promoting a socially conservative form of Islam (Ashton and Balci 2013; Zalewski 2013). Such criticism, others argue, is based on unsubstantiated fears with no evidence to support them (Ebaugh 2010; Özdalga 2003; Pandya and Gallagher 2012). These claims of a hidden political and/or religious agenda intrigued us, and that possibility became part of our cross-cultural investigation.

Past Studies and This One

Many past studies on the Gülen/Hizmet schools mostly have been descriptive in their analyses, either discussing them generally (Hendrick 2013; Pandya and Gallagher 2012; Yavuz 1999) or as operating in a specific country (Krauthamer 2012; Andrews 2011; Clement 2011; Lacey 2009). In examining schools run by followers of Gülen in Albania, Agai (2002) interviewed teachers to learn how their Islamic values guided their motivation to share humanistic values with their students. In her ethnographic research of Hizmet schools in Kazakhstan, Turam (2004) also interviewed teachers and administrators with a similar purpose in mind.

Generally, researchers have not studied these schools comparatively, seeking to discover—from multiple perspectives in different countries—exactly what impact, political or otherwise, these schools have on student and parental attitudes, behaviors and goals. A cross-cultural comparison thus provides context for our primary research objective to examine the effectiveness and impact of the movement's avowed objective to promote dialogue, tolerance and respect among different cultural and religious groups.

Through our interviews we also sought to determine how the motivations and reactions of individuals correspond to the schools' mission. Further, we wanted to know if, in the manifest and latent functions operative in integrating tradition with modernity and democracy, the schools also advanced a more specific political or religious agenda, as some critics have charged.

We investigated each school's organization, policies, curriculum, classroom resources, academic achievements, student and parent perceptions, teacher motivations and administrators' roles. Of particular interest were the means by which instilling such values were direct or through "implicit pedagogy" (Bourdieu and Passeron 1990). What exactly was taught in the classroom and what value lessons were communicated outside it? Naturally, we expected that the latter might be more effective among dorm students living 24/7 in a "total institution," where an enclosed, isolated social system exercises greater control over residents' lives (Goffman 1961).

Theoretical Influence

A theoretical construct guiding our research, at least in part, was negotiated order theory (Strauss 1978). Relevant to our interests was the emphasis on how, through social interaction, meaning is created and maintained through the structure and processes within an organization to achieve stated goals. For the Hizmet schools these goals were: 1) teaching modern, scientific and technological knowledge, and 2) promoting the universal human values of empathy and respect.

This theory suggests that the structural context goes beyond the limited organizational setting of the schools to encompass larger transcending practices. National issues (cultural, economic, governmental, historical, political or scientific) can affect conditions pertinent to the phenomena under study (Clarke 1991). By examining firsthand schools in different countries, we sought to explore what impact, if any, the external conditions of differing socio-historical realities had upon the operative processes (Strauss 1978, Geist and Hardesty 1992, Geist 1995).

What makes this interplay of external cultural influences of different countries upon the schools even more intriguing is the *intercultural* encounters *within* the schools. After all, these private educational institutions are initially set up by Turks and staffed by non-native teachers. Moreover, the longer the schools are in operation, the more likely they will have international students and/or enrollees of different religious backgrounds. Consequently, everyday interactions usually occur within a "specific social context involving intercultural communicators with specific role relationships, expectations, and behavioral norms and rules" (Kim 1988: 19). This is important because the schools may share a common philosophy and pedagogical approach, but they operate within different cultural settings and usually contain culturally diverse populations.

Negotiated order theory, therefore, is helpful in directing our attention to the interplay between social structures or social orders and students' patterns of participation within these structures. In other words, structure and interaction cannot be separated, for both play a vital role in the negotiating of a social order to work out the "concerted action" (Strauss 1978; Eisenberg and Riley 1988; Corbin 1991).

Research Methodology

Spending about a week in each country, we made an appointment with each school's chief administrator to learn about the school, gain his trust about our research plan, secure private rooms for our interviews, and gain access to students, teachers, and parents whom we selected. With each, we conducted semi-structured interviews. Whenever possible, we also sought out businessmen who were financial supporters, and these interviews always took place off site.

With administrators, parents, and financial supporters, the two of us conducted joint interviews. To interview as many teachers, students, and alumni within the limited time frames at each school, we split up and conducted those interviews one-on-one and later compared notes. We conducted our interviews at Hizmet schools in Tirana, Sarajevo, Almaty, Astana, Bucharest, Warsaw, Toronto, and Wayne, New Jersey in the United States. These schools varied from about 200 to more than 500 enrollees. Included were both same-sex and coed schools in all countries, as well as schools that had only dorm students, or no resident students at all, or a mixture of the two.

Given our time constraints and other challenges, we used stratified sampling to divide our student population by gender, religion, and year level, and our parent population by religion and social class (as primarily determined by occupation). We then used convenience sampling to secure not only our student and parent interviewees, but also our teacher and financial supporter interviewees.

All interviews were conducted in a private room and respondents were informed of our IRB-approved research guidelines and assured of the anonymity of their answers and their school affiliation. These in-depth, one-on-one interviews averaged a half hour, and were mostly conducted in English, but some parent interviews required use of an interpreter.

Our contextual questions probed into demographics, self-perceptions and institutional perceptions, the level of school and community involvement, and, from students, their personal experiences, academic aspirations, and future life goals. Other open-ended questions gave respondents the opportunity to expand further upon their comments, which we encouraged, as well as on other aspects of their social situations. When necessary, we asked pertinent follow-up questions.

To learn the objectives, structure and processes at the schools, we interviewed financial supporters, administrators, and teachers. To gain insights into how well these stated goals were achieved, we interviewed students and their parents. Among the more than 300 interviewees were 35 elementary or high school administrators, 28 elementary/ high school teachers, 140 middle-school and high-school students, 40 parents of high school students, 62 undergraduate and graduate students, and eight alumni. At several informal gatherings, either one-on-one or in groups of two, we also engaged 16 financial supporters in dialogue about their reasons for funding these schools.

Our choice of culturally distinct countries—each of them also comprised of differing demographic compositions and socioeconomic characteristics—provided an interesting context in which to study the societal impact on the Hizmet schools. Moreover, the countries' contrasting cultures and histories—some still evolving from Nazi and/or communist rule, unlike others with only a democratic past—offered further opportunities for comparative analysis.

The plan of this book is first to offer a societal context of each country in which the visited Hizmet schools operate. Next will be a profile of those schools, followed by interviews with administrators, teachers and staff, students, parents, and financial supporters. Each chapter closes with commentary on how apparent commonalities in structure and process are nonetheless impacted in their efforts and public acceptance either because of, or in spite of, cultural differences.

References

Agai, Bekim. 2002. "Fethullah Gülen and his Movement's Islamic Ethic of Education." *Critical Middle Eastern Studies* 11(1): 27-47.

Andrews, Mathew. 2011. "Building Institutional Trust in Germany: Relative Success of the Gülen and Milli Görüs." *Turkish Studies* 12(3): 511-524.

Ashton, Loye, and Tamer Balci, "A Contextual Analysis of the Supporters and Critics of the Gülen/Hizmet Movement." Retrieved March 1, 2021 (http://www.academia.edu/ 7467562/A_Contextual_Analysis_of_the_Supporters_and_Critics_of_the_G%C3%BClen_Hizmet_Movement).

Balci, Tamer, and Christopher L. Miller. 2012. *The Gülen Hizmet Movement: Circumspect Activism in Faith-Based Reform* (Newcastle upon Tyne, UK: Cambridge Scholars Publishing).

Bourdieu, Pierre, and Jean-Claude Passeron. 1990. *Reproduction in Education, Society and Culture*, 2d ed. (Thousand Oaks, CA: Sage Publications).

Çelik, Süleyman, "Bringing Up Peace Advocators Through Education: Gülen Movement Schools." *Journal of Arts, Science and Commerce* 8:4 (October 2017):29-38.

Çetin, Muhammed. 2007. "The Gülen Movement: Its Nature and Identity." Pp. 377-390 in İhsan Yılmaz, ed. *Muslim World in Transition: Contributions of the Gülen Movement*. London: Leeds Metropolitan University Press.

Clarke, A. E. 1991. "Social Worlds/Arenas Theory as Organizational Theory." Pp. 128-135 in D. R. Maine, ed. *Social Organization* and *Social Process: Essays in Honor of Anselm Strauss* (New York: Aldine De Gruyter).

Clement, Victoria. 2011. "Faith-Based Schools in Post-Soviet Turkmenistan," *European Education* 43(Spring): 76-92.

Corbin, J. M. 1991. "Anselm Strauss: An Intellectual Biography." Pp. 17-41 in D. R. Maines, ed. *Social Organization and Social Processes: Essays in Honor of Anselm Strauss* (New York: Aldine De Gruyter).

Ebaugh, Helen R. 2010. *The Gülen Movement: A Sociological Analysis of Civic Movement Rooted in Modern Islam* (New York: Springer).

Eisenberg, E. M. and Riley, P. 1988. "Organizational Symbols and Sense-Making." pp. 131-150, in M. Goldhaber and G. A. Barnett, eds. *Handbook of Organizational Communication* (Norwood, NJ: Ablex).

Eldridge, Bruce. 2007. "Gülen's Educational Philosophy." Paper given at the 2007 Conference on Muslim World in Transition: Contributions of the Gülen Movement, London.

Ergene, M. Enes. 2008. *Tradition Witnessing the Modern Age* (Somerset, NJ: Tughra Press).

Facts of File. 1992. "Major US Racial Disturbances since 1965." Facts on File, 52 (May 7): 328.

Geist, P. 1995. "Negotiating Whose Order? Communicating to Negotiate Identities and Revise Organizational Structures." Pp. 43-63 in A. M. Nicotera, ed. *Conflict in Organizations: Communicative Processes* (New York: SUNY Press).

Geist, Patricia and Hardesty, Monica. 1992. *Negotiating the Crisis: Drugs and the Transformation of Hospitals* (Hillsdale, NJ: Lawrence Erlbaum).

Goffman, Erving. 1961. *Asylum: Essays on the Social Situation of Mental*

Patients (New York: Anchor Books/Doubleday).

Gülen, Fethullah. 1996. *Towards the Lost Paradise*. London: Truestar.

Gülen, Fethullah. 2004. *Pearls of Wisdom* (Clifton, NJ: Tughra Books).

Gülen, Fethullah. 2006. "Our System of Education." Retrieved March 1, 2021 (https://pearls.org/golden-keys/towards-the-lost-paradise/97-our-system-of-education.html).

Gülen, Fethullah. 2010. *Toward a Global Civilization of Love and Tolerance* (Clifton, NJ: Tughra Books).

Hansen, Suzy. 2012. "The Global Imam," *New Republic* 241:19 (December 2): 10-15.

Hendrick, Joshua D. 2013. *Gülen: The Ambiguous Politics of Market Islam in Turkey and the World* (New York: NYU Press).

Judd, Emily and Lauren Holtmeier, "Why Is Turkey's Erdoğan Persecuting the Gülen Movement?" *Al Arabiya* (June 10, 2020). Retrieved March 1, 2021 (https://english.alarabiya.net/en/features/2020/06/10/).

Kim, Young Yun. 1988 *Communication and Cross-Cultural Adaptation: An Interdisciplinary Theory* (Cleveland, England: Multilingual Matters).

Koç, Doğan. 2016. "Strategic Defamation of Fethullah Gülen: English vs. Turkish." *European Journal of Economic and Political Studies* 4:189–244.

Krauthamer, Ky. 2012. "In Albania, Madrasas Even the Secular Love." *Transitions Online*, 6.

Lacey, Jonathan. 2009. "The Gülen Movement in Ireland: Civil Society Engagements of a Turkish Religio-Cultural Movement." *Turkish Studies* 10:2 (June): 295-315.

Luttwak, Edward. 2016. "Erdoğan's Purge Is a Sectarian War." *Foreign Policy*, August 3. Retrieved March 1, 2021 (http://foreignpolicy.com/2016/08/03/erdogans-purge-is-a-sectarian-war-turkey-gulen/).

Mango, Andrew. 2005. "Religion and Culture in Turkey," *Middle Eastern Studies* 42:6: 997-1032.

Nelson, Charles. 2005. "Fethullah Gülen: A Vision of Transcendent Education," Retrieved March 1, 2021 (http://citeseerx.ist.psu.edu/viewdoc/download?doi=10.1.1.506.8605&rep=rep1&type=pdf).

Özdalga, Elisabeth. 2003. "Secularizing Trends in Fethullah Gülen's

Movement: Impasse or opportunity for Further Renewal?" *Critique: Critical Middle Eastern Studies* 42 (Spring): 61-73.

Pandya, Sophia, and Nancy Gallagher. 2012. *The Gülen Hizmet Movement and Its Transnational Activities: Case Studies of Altruistic Activism in Contemporary Islam* (Boca Raton, FL: Brown Walker Press).

Strauss, Anselm. 1978. *Negotiations: Varieties, Contexts; Processes, and Social Order* (San Francisco: Jossey-Bass).

Tittensor, David. 2014. *The House of Service: The Gülen Movement and Islam's Third Way.* New York: Oxford University Press.

Turam, Berna. 2004. "A Bargain Between the Secular State and Turkish Islam: Politics of Ethnicity in Central Asia." *Nations and Nationalism* 10 (3): 353-374.

Turam, Berna. 2007. *Between Islam and the State: The Politics of Engagement.* Stanford, CA: Stanford University Press.

Ünal, Ali, and Alphonse Williams, eds. 2000. *Advocate of Dialogue* (Fairfax, VA: The Fountain).

Watmough, Simon P., and Ahmet Erdi Öztürk. 2018. "From 'Diaspora by Design' to Transnational Political Exile: The Gülen Movement in Transition." *Politics, Religion & Ideology* 19 (May): 33-52.

Yavuz, M. Hakan. 1999. "Towards an Islamic Liberalism? The Nurcu Movement and Fethullah Gülen." *Middle East Journal* 53:4 (Autumn): 584-605.

Yildirim, Y. 2004. 'Fethullah Gülen's Golden Generation: Integration of Muslim Identity with the World Through Education.' Paper presented at Association of Muslim Social Scientists of North America annual conference at George Mason University, Virginia, September 2004.

Zalewski, Piotr. 2013. "Turkey's Erdoğan Battles Country's Most Powerful Religious Movement," *Time World*, December 4. Retrieved March 1, 2021 (http://world.time. com/2013/12/04/turkeys-erdogan-battles-with-countrys-most-powerful-religious-movement/).

2

Bosnia & Herzegovina

This country seemed an excellent one with which to begin our cross-cultural study. If key elements in the Gülen movement are not only respect and tolerance for all faiths but also, and even more importantly, interfaith dialogue, then what better place to measure the effectiveness of the Hizmet schools than in the land where, in the 1990s, the brutality of religious "ethnic cleansing" resulted in widespread suffering, devastation, and killings?

The Sarajevo valley is surrounded by the rugged snow-capped peaks of the Dinaric Alps. Their natural beauty offers no sign of the manmade interethnic savagery that had riddled this region two decades earlier. Yet from those same mountains almost completely surrounding the city, Serbian forces had continually bombarded it with mortar shells, killing thousands of civilians. In the Markale open market in the heart of the city, one can see a preserved impact crater, now painted red to memorialize the 43 people killed from a 1995 shelling. Elsewhere are similarly marked small craters, as well as many bullet holes in buildings throughout the city. These reminders of the recent past offer cause for wonder if they continue to have a positive or negative effect on the current state of interethnic relations. We would soon learn that psychic scars still remain among many older adults, but among the younger generation—who are not taught about the war in school and commonly not at home either—neutrality appears to exist about the past, at least in the students' expressed thoughts.

Although still bearing some of the physical scars of war two decades later, Sarajevo was undergoing a building boom at the time of our visit. That boom increased even more so since, especially in hotels, fueled by an unprecedented growth in its tourism that had been expanding yearly until the coronavirus pandemic curtailed travel in 2020 (Reuters 2020).

We saw many signs of new construction, as well as positive reminders of what this pluralistic society once was like. Before the divisiveness of interethnic warfare, Sarajevo—thanks to its rich history of peaceful cultural diversity—enjoyed a reputation as "the Jerusalem of Europe." One visual evidence of those bygone years is a mosque, synagogue, Catholic church, and Eastern Orthodox church situated within a two-block radius of one another.

Societal Overview

With a population of nearly 3.9 million, Bosnia and Herzegovina (often referred to as BiH in numerous publications) was facing a difficult economic transition. Metal industries remained the backbone of its manufacturing sector, but tourism (cultural, historical, skiing, and eco-adventures) was then rapidly increasing (UNWTO 2018). When we were there in 2014, high unemployment (44 percent among adults 25 and older, and 63 percent among 15 to 24) was a serious concern, despite a literary rate of 99 percent. Until the pandemic caused massive layoffs, those unemployment numbers had been cut in half by 2019 (*CIA World Factbook* 2020).

Bosniaks (Bosnian Muslims) are the largest ethnic group at 50 percent, followed by Serbs (31 percent) and Croats (15 percent). This Balkan country was once a model multicultural society with its diverse groups peacefully living side by side for generations and with high religious intermarriage rates (Petersen 2011:246). Today, in the aftermath of the interethnic conflict of a generation ago, one manifestation of the divisiveness still permeating in Bosnia and Herzegovina is its unusual arrangement of a shared national presidency among the three ethnic groups that rotates every eight months.

Given the country's tumultuous history of war and "ethnic cleansing," religion remains, not surprisingly, important in people's lives. Among Bosniaks, more than three-fourths said that religion was an important part of their daily lives, while more than a third said it was "very important." Although only 10 percent said they never attend a mosque, many others don't go regularly either. Just 30 percent reported that they worship in a mosque at least once a week, and only 18 percent said they prayed at least several times a day. Among Bosnians of all faiths, 54 percent say religion is very important in their lives, far more than in Albania (15 percent) and Kazakhstan (22 percent), countries to be discussed in the next two chapters (Pew Research 2019, 2012).

Schools

Ten years of primary education, beginning at age six, is compulsory and free. It is batched in four-year cycles: ages six to nine, nine to twelve, twelve to fifteen. Secondary education, beginning at age fifteen is also free and typically lasts for three years, resulting in most youth graduating when they are eighteen or nineteen. In Bosnia and Herzegovina, as in many other countries, a secondary school is called a *college*, thereby giving the term a different connotation than in the United States. The private Hizmet schools, which are not free as are the public schools, do not necessarily follow the same grade structure, as we discovered with our first visit, but all of them are recognized by the BiH Ministry of Education.

The first Hizmet school opened in 1996 in Sarajevo. In less than two decades, five primary schools and three high schools were operating in one of five Albanian cities (Bihac, Mostar, Sarajevo, Tuzla and Zenica). We found that three education institutions—International Burch University, Sarajevo College, and Una Sana College—also functioned within the scope of Bosna Sema Educational Institutions, the umbrella organization that assists and supports all of these privately owned schools, all operating with the approval of the country's Ministry of Education.

Sarajevo Koledz, which began in 1996, has 250 enrolled male students in grades K to 5, and another 250 students in grades six to nine. Located on a beautiful campus in Sokolovic Kolonija, one of the Sarajevo neighborhoods, it has a dormitory, although commuter students also attend. School enrollment consists of 30 nationalities, and about 20 percent of the high school students are on scholarship. The selectivity in student admissions is clear in the following numbers: a total of 10,000 primary school graduates takes the entrance exam; of the 2,000 finalists with high scores, only 50 are selected, strictly based on those test scores.

At the girls-only International School of Sarajevo were 250 students enrolled in grades nine through twelve. Like the boys at Sarajevo
College, the girls were the selective few chosen for their high scores on
the entrance exam, and 20 percent of them were on scholarship. Their
school, which also has a dormitory, is on a mountain overlooking the
city of Sarajevo. The classroom building—with a ground-floor cafeteria—was pockmarked with bullet holes and stood as an empty shell
until Bosna Sema took possession, renovated it, and added a floor to
make it three stories high. The staff includes a principal, vice principal,
school counselor, dormitory director, and twelve teachers, two of them
male.

In a question we asked each administrator about the school's
mission and goals, we did find a philosophic universality, perhaps best
summed up by this high school vice principal:

Our goal is social harmony, building for the future. We look for
smart children, even in small villages, to give them an opportunity to
learn, through scholarships. One day they will give back, not to us, but
to the country.

Teachers

We interviewed four teachers, two males and two females, all Bosniaks.
Actually, one of the women taught only part time. She had a Ph.D. degree,
had been a social worker since 1997, and now was on the staff at the girls'
school where her daughter was a sophomore. She offered two insights
into what we were learning about some of the practices in this country.
She had lived through the Bosnian war of 1992-1995, and her comments,
we discovered, would reflect those of other interviewed adults:

> The country is still in transition, and we all face the burden of change.
> We all must get involved. We cannot make progress if children are
> burdened by the past, so we do not talk about the war in our fam-
> ilies and we do not study it in our schools. If we follow democracy,
> we must offer more and conduct ourselves to meet the needs of our
> children…. We must bring Islam and democracy together. We must
> adjust to modern society and realize everyone's ambitions. We must
> instill and bring something positive to other parts of the country.

She was quite passionate in expressing this emphasis on a hopeful future and not the unpleasant past. On the practice of teachers visiting homes and of their extra-curricular tea-time sessions with students (to be explained later), she informed us that it is a Balkan tradition to share meals, and this practice thereby provides better connections and communication between teachers and parents, and between teachers and students.

These two strands of thought also permeated the remarks of a twenty-six-year-old teacher of English, who had graduated from the University of Sarajevo, a public university, two years earlier.

> There was no winner in the war, and now each group is writing its own history. Serbians and Croatians have home countries, and nationalism is pulling the country apart. We Bosniaks have only Bosnia and we are trying to hold the country together. The tripartite system is dysfunctional and people are demoralized. We need to teach our young people to respect, not fear, each other.

This idealistic young man, who had graduated from the very high school in which he was now teaching, saw himself as needing to pay forward the "gift" he had been given, by communicating "positive thoughts and energy to the next generation."

> This school helped me to create myself as a person to help myself. God knows where I would be if I didn't go to this school. Here there is no hierarchy; we are all friends. To make this world a better place, I must help young people to become more aware of problems around them. There is no place for selfishness. We must all sacrifice for the common good.

A biology teacher, apparently in her forties, held advanced degrees from Croatia and Turkey. She expressed admiration for the organization, its contact with students, and the ways they are stimulated to learn by working on projects. Then she identified key differences between public schools and a private Hizmet school:

> The problem in the state schools is the teachers must furnish everything. There is less learning because the teachers typically do not adapt to students, but here there are more interactive relations with teachers plus cross-generational activity outside the school.

Her statements on how the school inculcated positive value orientations about diversity were unique in their expression, but similar to others' views. She continued:

> Our students learn to know and understand if there are differences in people, these are good things not bad things. There is no difference here in how we look and talk, as we do our part to end the social segregation that keeps us apart.

The comments of another graduate of the University of Sarajevo, a math teacher who had four years' teaching experience, perhaps encapsulates the motivations and views of all the teachers that we met:

> I came here at first because of the languages, but then I discovered how everyone helps each other, just like family. Everyone is so kind, and not jealous if someone else is good at something. So, I wanted to teach in a school like this. I'm glad to be part of it, doing something for my country. Elsewhere, kids are sometimes scared of teachers who are not friendly. Students need to love you, to trust you. They need encouragement, confidence. Then they can trust other people. Here, we lead by example. Elsewhere teachers may not talk to students outside the classroom.

As we would discover in our travels to other Hizmet schools, these altruistic and idealistic goals, along with the desire to have students excel in their studies, would be the norm among the teachers, regardless of their faith or cultural background.

Students

On the first of our two days at the coeducational International High School of Sarajevo, we seized upon an unexpected opportunity to conduct a focus group discussion with seven boys—six Bosniaks (Muslims) and one Bosnian Christian. They had just returned from successfully competing in an international academic Olympiad in Houston, Texas, winning several medals, and they were concluding a celebratory, school-sponsored dinner in their honor. We had arrived for an orientation tour of the facility before interviewing other students and teachers the next day, but the school officials agreed to our impromptu request to speak to them. It was clear in time we spent with them that they liked and respected each other, and religion had no relevance in their relationships. As a prelude to the one-on-one interviews with perhaps "less stellar" students the next day, we wanted to get a sense of these students' attitudes first. We led a discussion among them on two topics: what they liked best about their school and what values they thought they had learned at the school.

Quickly emerging as a shared attitude about this school was these students' admiration for their "very special" teachers as they called them, more particularly their "behavior." To illustrate, they spoke to a strong bond they felt of caring and interconnectedness. The teachers had visited their homes, bringing their own families with them, for all to get to know one another. Their teachers were willing to stay after school to help them with their lessons. Teachers made a point of becoming familiar with each student, so someone doing poorly would be helped, and they also encouraged students to help one another. As one student put it, "They help us understand the process of learning; they are not just interested in the results."

On the question about values learned, two themes emerged. "We learn to be self-reliant," said one. The others nodded in agreement, as another said, "Yes we learn to be independent, but we also learn teamwork." A third student added, "We spend time together with our classmates and we learn to cooperate with each other." That continuing discussion led to many comments about another learned value that all enthusiastically discussed.

"We've learned to have relationships with people unlike us," began this part of the discussion as another student stated, "Yes, here we've met other cultures and learned to be tolerant and to live with them." Soon all of them wanted to speak about this. "This institution makes you more tolerant." "You learn to accept others." "Well, yes, we should accept others, but not if they are doing something wrong. Then we should tell them to help them improve their character."

And so, the group discussion went on for two hours. We left that evening impressed by their morale and fervent endorsement of their school and its teachers. We looked forward to our interviews the next day when we interviewed randomly selected other students to learn how widely shared were such views.

The six students interviewed at length the next day did indeed echo those sentiments, each in their own way. An eighteen-year-old young man whose interests were math and playing soccer said, "I like most the relationships between students and teachers. They are always helping and asking if you need something. My sister is in a public school and this doesn't exist there." As to values learned, he replied,

> You can learn a lot of things, but for me, it's the making of good people, good morals. We learn these values by the process; the teachers are role models. I've learned to help others, not just think of myself. Now I have many non-Muslim friends.

A nineteen-year-old, also a senior on full scholarship because of his entrance test scores and consistent high grades, spoke of having non-Muslim friends and liking his teachers: "The teachers are like our friends. We have picnics together and they go to our homes." He had studied English since the third grade and hoped to major in electrical engineering at a U.S. university. He lived in the dorms, but offered, "There is a real community here, even with non-residents, and we all learn right from wrong by seeing others, seeing other people's actions but also their reactions."

Another eighteen-year-old senior, planning to become a computer programmer, liked how the school helped students of different cultures integrate with one another, lamenting about the division still in his country: "The Serbians won't even carry the Bosnian flag!" He was the only Christian student (Croatian Orthodox) we interviewed, and he spoke of having problems his first year—experiencing mocking and prejudice—but how he and others learned openness from their student life experiences and now his best friend is a Muslim.

A nineteen-year-old senior was rather effusive in his comments:

> I like our teachers' character, their altruism and self-sacrifice, their open communication. They help us and they come to our homes. They are interested in what we think, what we are reading, what message comes out of the knowledge. They are not just our teachers—there is a friendship. All of them are the same.

His remarks about values instilled in him as he neared completion of high school years were equally compelling:

We can all be moderate; tolerance is possible by example. Islam and democracy are important. We are learning what we can give our people. By teaching us to work with other people, they are creating a new generation, like a flower. My friends from before are more materialistic and do not see the bigger picture of helping others. If you don't change yourself, it will not change your situation.

Sharing a comparable attitude was this seventeen-year-old junior:

My family gave me good values but this school improved me. Here I learned good study habits but also how to behave, be a better person. We are all the same people. I know because now I have non-Muslim friends. It is important what we have here [points to head] AND [his emphasis] here [points to heart].

Would female high school students hold similar viewpoints? We were about to learn from the next set of interviews at the International School of Sarajevo. In its cafeteria where we ate lunch, very few students wore the *hijab*. We were able to secure a bit more diversity among our interviewees. In particular, a Chinese student piqued our curiosity and we were intrigued to hear what she had to say. She was eighteen years old, in her third year, and an only child whose father was a shopkeeper with a college degree and whose mother had a high school education and worked with him. Completely unaware of the Gülen movement or the nature of its schools, she and her parents had picked this school "because it is the best school. It has biology, math, physics—and I want to learn, then go on to a U.S. university to study chemistry and psychology." Comments about her education paralleled what we already had heard from the boys: "The teachers are close to us, and so are the older students. There is love between others. I have friends from different countries and we are very close together."

A senior Christian female who commutes to school exemplified the harmonious religious diversity that once existed in this part of the world; her aunt is Muslim. Both of her parents are high school graduates and her father is a TV cameraman. *[We would later arrange to interview her father.]* She had taken the entrance exam, as do all accepted students, and won a scholarship that continued throughout high school due to her high grades, and she recently received a scholarship to attend Burch University, where she plans to study English. Her statements were also complimentary:

> It's really different here. We have friendly relations with the teachers. They're mostly young and they are just like friends.... This school really changed me. I started to care more about other people, not just myself. We help each other out. For example, the upper classmen help the lower.

A freshman, age 16, was a Muslim who commuted, on a 50 percent scholarship, and planned to be a teacher. The only child of a college-educated engineer father and a mother who had only a high school education but worked as a family consultant, she too reflected on Bosnia's harmonious ethnic past in that she had a cousin who married a Catholic. Her remarks personified, as we would learn, what the war-ravaged older generation was attempting to pass on to the next generation:

> Religion is a personal thing only that person should know. I am more interested in democracy. I'm not too young. We are the ones mixing nationality and religion.

For that reason, she liked the school enabling everyone to meet other cultures to "widen their vision."

Two other commuting students, both Muslims, had parents with high school educations and were attending because they had won scholarships. One student's father owned a driving school and the other's father was a metalworker. Like their fellow students, they also had university ambitions and, in separate interviews, each praised their teachers' abilities and exceptional rapport with students. Perhaps more importantly, they spoke to the values they were learning with full awareness of the ethnocide that had occurred just before they were born.

> Bosnia is a small country and it's important we learn not to think only of ourselves so we can make it better.... I am now more friendly to others since coming here.

> The friendly atmosphere offers more than studying. Here we have more opportunities to interact closely with other cultures.... We get to understand people better. We need the unity; we are all Bosnians.

We need to look for a better perspective, have patience, help each other, give things freely, become more social to cooperate with peo-ple—share and say things—no talking behind others' backs—have the opportunity to be different—do something.

Even greater diversity awaited us at the International School of Sarajevo. Our student interviews included a Bosnian Orthodox, Hun-garian Catholic, Iranian Baha'i, Iranian Muslim, Saudi Muslim, and two Bosnian Muslims. We interviewed four males and three females, rang-ing in age from a precocious, highly verbal eleven-year-old (an advanced placement freshman) to eighteen-year-old seniors. Four had college-ed-ucated parents, and two were the children of diplomats stationed in this country. All planned to go on to a university; those with known intended majors identified them as architecture, genetics and bioengineering, po-litical science, or psychology.

Once again, despite their different backgrounds, we heard compli-ments from all the students about their teachers. This group, in their pri-vate interviews, also mentioned friendly relationships, competent teach-ing, and helpfulness as reasons for their testimonials. However, several students made a distinction between more supportive Turkish teachers and some less-so Bosnian teachers. One troubling matter was the claim by two students that evolution was not taught in their biology class and that one of them was penalized good conduct points for "lying" after complaining about the omission. Yet two other students who had taken biology insisted that evolution was part of their biology class, although it was with a different instructor. This was the only instance of such an assertion, whether here in Bosnia and Herzegovina or in other schools we would visit over the next three years.

Besides everyone liking their teachers, students volunteered feel-ings about the school environment. These included classes in English, required uniforms "so everyone is equal and there are no concerns about what to wear," a good curriculum, and the presence of many foreign stu-dents. One student, smaller in stature than his classmates, was especially thankful that the school was "very strict about bullying and fighting." However, another student also shorter than his classmates spoke about being bullied and beaten up by a few students in his first year because he was new and not a Muslim. And yet, he said that by his third year, he "became best friends with some of those bullies." A third student said that some students first made fun of him because he was a Christian, but no longer did so.

Perhaps that change in two years in these students' experiences from aggressive to pleasant relationships was an outgrowth of the values that educators tried to instill. "Here we learn to live with other cultures," said a Muslim junior. "I am more friendly to others since coming here," reported an Orthodox senior. "We learn good behavior besides our subjects," a Muslim sophomore told us. "They show us that one's character is found in behavior, such as not cheating, stealing, lying, or harming others," noted another Muslim student.

Teenage conflicts are common in most private or public high schools in any country, and school administrators everywhere do their best to contain and resolve them. Utilizing both a behavioral point system and a conscious effort in character-building through educator role models, the Hizmet schools possibly address issues of bullying and fighting more completely than many other educational institutions. At least we saw more indicators of such attempts than we have seen in countless non-Hizmet schools in the course of our professional lives.

Parents

The eight parents we interviewed had spent their childhood in pre-war Bosnia with its interreligious harmony and with religious intermarriages in many of their own families. They had spent their late teens and/or early twenties amid the fighting, bombing, and mass killings. We were therefore interested to learn what they had to say about their children enrolled in Hizmet schools that emphasized respect, understanding, and acceptance of the "other."

"My daughter never came home offended because of her religion; she even received Christmas presents from her Muslim teachers," said a Serbian Orthodox single mother of two teenage girls, ages 15 and 17.

"Here they teach to respect each other, even if not the same," another mother observed. A Bosniak woman who did not wear the *hijab*, she added, "They learn responsibility for others and to care about other people. They gain the concept of teamwork by working together on projects in their classes."

A Muslim father whose only child, a daughter, attended the international school, declared that he liked philosophy of the school because she learns new cultures and to accept them. Similarly, a Bosnian Catholic mother noted that, despite religious and cultural differences, her daughter had changed for the better, opening herself more to be friendlier, after realizing all were same in personality and behavior.

Our most poignant parent interview was with a TV cameraman who was a Christian. He sent his daughter to the girls' high school because a friend of hers already attended the school and liked it. Most important to him was she would study in English, and he learned the teachers were more intimate with students, more available, in contrast to the public schools where "they just do their job and nothing else." But it was what he tearfully told us next that was so moving:

> Before the war, all people were friends, not looking at faith. We never felt there was a problem. I didn't even know what they were. It wasn't important. Then it all changed terribly. When my daughter came here, and what she learned and what I saw, I rediscovered some of those old feelings. I said to my wife, any school that can do that, bring us together again, I want to support, and I do. It is not easy for us financially, but I am now an investor in this school and I recommend it to all my Christian friends.

Regarding other elements of the school, the parents were in general agreement about the quality of their child's school, the close connections between teachers and students, and the safe environment. A Bosniak father, holding a high position in his profession, thought the educators had "honest intentions and desired to achieve the very best from each student." He especially liked the "holistic approach the school uses in which teachers and families socialize and there is full communication on students so there is a common understanding of their education."

A Bosniak father discussed how pleased he was that all students receive the same treatment, with no special privileges for children of the elite as in the state schools:

> All are helped and help, even the gifted ones. If a student is falling back, there are special activities to help. This is very important in the

raising of a child, because sometimes the parents get confused about some of these subjects.

A Bosniak mother's comments accentuated those just mentioned:

> There are all smart girls in her class, only 20 out of 4,000 [total applicants]. Even so, there is no competition among them. All help each other, love each other. I mean, there is no jealousy. Such a thing is not normal for me. I don't know how she does it.

From their collective comments, it was easy to recognize that parental satisfaction crossed numerous, potentially dividing, boundaries—particularly religion and social class.

Financial Supporters

Over pre-arranged breakfast or dinner meetings in all three countries, we met with businessmen who had provided initial and continuing financial support for these schools, both in operating expenses and scholarships. All of them were highly successful businessmen, either as developers, distributors, manufacturers, or owners of other lucrative company enterprises. Each was committed to the third pillar of Islam, *zakat*, fulfilling the obligation of all financially stable Muslims to be charitable through acts done without publicity, to keep the action pure. Thus, no schools, buildings or building sections are named after major investors.

When asked why he gave so much money to the Turkish schools, a businessman in Bosnia gave the simple reply, "Humanity." When pressed to explain, he added,

I invest in the future, in a better world, as these schools produce educated people who appreciate the humanity in all people no matter how different they are.

International Burch University

Another part of the Bosna Sema Educational Institutions family, the University began in 2008, and it is situated on a small campus in the Ilidza section of Sarajevo. Except for courses in Turkish language and literature, all classes are taught in English. It has three Faculties— Education, Economics and Social Sciences, Engineering & Information Technologies—comprising ten academic departments. Accredited by the BiH Ministry of Education and offering seven baccalaureate degrees and twelve advanced degrees, the University had a combined enrollment of nearly 3,000 undergraduate and graduate students.

Although most of the high school students we interviewed planned to study elsewhere, a few did plan to attend this university, including two who had recently received scholarships. Although we did not have time to interview any currently enrolled students, we were curious to see the facilities. We found that the modern buildings contained well-equipped classrooms.

Retrospect

Our first series of visits and interviews in Bosnian Hizmet schools provided positive testimony from multiple perspectives by those directly involved. Comments from administrators, teachers, students, and parents at three different schools reinforced one another. In response to our subtle questioning on the matter, no one even suggested the existence of a political or religious agenda, but the common thread of the promotion of intercultural and interpersonal acceptance was clearly evident. Also notable in the comments was how this country's cultural history played a role in how the adults—educators and especially parents—identified with the schools and their joint mission.

Of course, no institution is perfect and not all teachers are ideal models. That biology teacher, one who not only rejected evolution but punished a student for his intellectual challenge to that position, was not just an unfortunate rarity. He seemed, at least to this writer, to be a counter-image to what the Hizmet schools promote in scientific knowledge, as well as respect and tolerance for the other.

Despite this one sour note, our field research in Bosnia and Herzegovina revealed many positive dimensions to the schools we visited. Because our intent was to draw comparisons through a cross-cultural study, we looked forward to visiting the Hizmet schools in Albania, where about three-fourths of the population are Muslims, compared to about half in this country.

References

"Bosnia and Herzegovina." 2020. *CIA Word Factbook*. Retrieved March 1, 2021 (https://www.cia.gov/ library/publications/the-world-fact-book/geos/bk.html).

Peterson, Roger D. 2011. *Western Intervention in the Balkans: The Strategic Use of Emotion in Conflict* (New York: Cambridge University Press).

Pew Research Center. 2018. "Eastern/Western Europeans Differ on Importance of Religion, Views of Minorities, and Key Social Issues." Retrieved March 1, 2021 (https://www.pewforum.org/2018/10/29/eastern-and-western-europeans-differ-on-importance-of-religion-views-of-minorities-and-key-social-issues/).

Pew Research, Religion & Public Life Project. 2012. "The World's Muslims: Unity and Diversity." Retrieved March 1, 2021 (http://www.pewforum.org/2012/08/09/the-worlds-muslims-unity-and-diversity-2-religious-commitment/).

Reuters. 2020. "Coronavirus Cuts Bosnian Tourism by 70.6% in First Half of 2020." Retrieved March 1, 2021 (https://www.reuters.com/article/bosnia-tourism-idUSL8N2FC22M).

United Nations World Trade Organization. 2018. *Tourism Highlights*. Retrieved March 1, 2021 (https://www.e-unwto.org/doi/epdf/10.18111/9789284419876).

3

ALBANIA

Albania is a Balkan country located in southeastern Europe. Facing the Adriatic Sea above Greece, it has a population of three million and is one of the poorest countries on the continent. It suffers from a weak economy, high unemployment, an inadequate energy and transportation infrastructure, with widespread corruption and powerful organized crime networks (CIA World Factbook 2020). Albania has a high literacy rate (98 percent), but the average adult has 10 years of schooling (education is only compulsory through the ninth grade), less than all other countries we visited for this study (OECD 2020).

Societal Overview

Mostly homogeneous in nationality, the country contains about 86 percent Albanians. Greeks, Turks, Roma and Italians are the largest groups among the small number of minorities. The 2011 census identified Muslims as constituting about 57 percent of the total population but, in terms of family orientation rather than actual affiliation, the number changes to 76 percent. Other religious groups include Roman Catholics 10 percent, Orthodox 7 percent, and Bektashi (a Sufi order) 2 percent (CIA World Factbook 2020; Çela, et al. 2015:20).

Religion, however, appears not to be a major factor among Albanian Muslims. Only 15 percent view religion as "very important in their lives," the lowest percentage of all countries with significant Muslim populations. When controlled for age, the percentage drops for young adults, ages 18 to 34, to 11 percent, but rises to 19 percent for the 35-and-older cohort (Pew Research 2012). Another study of 114 countries ranked Albania as the thirteenth least religious country in the world and reported that only 39 percent of Albanians said religion was an "important part of daily life" (Gallup 2010).

Most likely, Albania's recent history is a major factor in these findings. In 1967, the communist government of Enver Hoxha closed 2,167 churches, mosques, monasteries, and other religious institutions and converted them into warehouses, gymnasiums, workshops or cultural centers. Further, he ordered the complete razing of all minarets at mosques and any tombstones with religious symbols in his zealous purge. Outlawing all religious practices, he declared Albania to be "the world's first atheist nation." The government renamed towns bearing religious names and forbade parents to give their children any names associated with a religious faith. Religious leaders were executed, forced into hard labor camps, or went into hiding (Moorey 2015).

After Hoxha's death in 1985, religious institutions reopened, but they no longer attracted large numbers. Albanians may identify with the Islamic, Orthodox, or Catholic roots of their families, but they seem to do so only to acknowledge their heritage and are not themselves religious. For example, 44 percent of Muslims reported that they never attend a mosque, women (52 percent) less likely to do so than men (36 percent). Even those who are practitioners mostly have a more secular interpretation of Islam than found in many other countries (Pew Research 2012).

In the early 1990s, following the collapse of communism in Albania, Turkish entrepreneurs began sponsoring the establishment of Gülen-inspired secular schools. They did so with the endorsement and support of the Turkish state, as evidenced by the presence of Turkey's Prime Minister at the time, Recep Tayyip Erdoğan, at the inauguration of Turgut Özal College's elementary school in Durres, on February 17, 2005. On a state visit to Albania in May 2015, though, his deteriorating relationship with Fethullah Gülen and his followers led Erdoğan, by then the Turkish President, to call for their closure as part of a "terrorist organization." His remarks sparked a barrage of criticism from Albanian politicians, including President Bujar Nishani, Interior Minister Saimir Tahiri, and Parliament Speaker Ilir Meta, all of whom rejected him, saying these institutions pay their taxes to the state and have provided education in line with the laws to thousands of Albanians (Cihan News Agency 2015).

Religious Schools

A strong indication of the ongoing support that Hizmet schools have received from the Albanian community is in the evolution of the madrasas (Islamic religious schools) that were established in Albania in the early 1990s with donations from Saudi Arabia and the United Arab Emirates. Although Saudi-financed madrasas have achieved some notoriety, especially in Pakistan for their teaching of Wahhabism (a particularly austere and rigid form of Islamic fundamentalism), researchers have found them to be promoters of social cohesion rather than purveyors of outgroup bias (Delavande and Zafar 2015; Myriam and Laura 2011).

When the Albanian madrasas lost their Arabic sponsors in the mid-1990s, senior officials of the Muslim community sought to save these schools. Their logical choice was the Gülen Cemaat [religious community] whose schools already enjoyed significant esteem for their quality. They approached the Sema Foundation (Fondacioni Sema), the local umbrella organization that provided support for the Gülen-inspired schools in Albania. Accepting such an offer would be a substantial departure from the prevailing philosophy and mission of the secular schools that emphasized adult role models and kind actions to build moral character, but not religious instruction.

Nonetheless, the Sema Foundation agreed and, in 1995, it began to operate co-jointly with the Komuniteti Musliman (Muslim Community) the first madrasa in Elbasan, one of the largest cities located in the center of the country. Absorption of the next madrasa from a Wahhabi group came three years later in Kavajë, a small city in the Western Lowlands. In 2005, a Qatari foundation surrendered its madrasa in the capital city of Tirana. Next was the madrasa in Berat, an old city in south-central Albania and, in 2010, the Foundation reconstructed the demolished madrasa in Korçë, one of the largest and most important cultural and economic centers of Albania, located in the southeastern part of the country (Öktem 2010).

On our visit to Tirana's madrasa, as we walked up the stairs to the office of the school's co-director, we immediately realized this was not a typical Muslim religious school, for it was coeducational. He greeted us and, as we sat down in comfortable chairs, we noted the Turkish and Albanian flags adjoining his desk. Like directors at all schools that we visited—religious or secular—he was a Turkish native. Over the al-ways-offered Turkish tea and pastries, he informed us that the school's 460 students followed a curriculum approved by the Education Minis-try, and that it emphasized English, computer skills, and science. Of the seven hours of daily classes, one hour is devoted to religious study of the Quran, including for the few Christian students at the school. (Only in the madrasas is religion taught, however; all other Hizmet schools are secular.) Almost all graduates continue their education at a university, most of them majoring in secular subjects.

As interesting as the madrasas proved to be, our research focus was on the secular Hizmet schools, and to them we now turn.

Secular Schools

The oldest of the Gulen-inspired schools in Albania is Mehmet Akif Col-lege (*Kolegji Mehmet Akif*), which opened in Tirana in 1993. Again, the reader should keep in mind that college does not have the same higher education connotation as it does in the United States.

Since 2009, Albania has had a 5-4-3 formal education structure. Its primary schools have an official entry age of six and five grades. Grades six through nine constitute the lower secondary schools, while the up-per secondary schools consist of grades ten through twelve (Education Policy and Data Center 2020). Thus, the term college can refer either to an educational institution that contains all three levels—as does Turgut Özal College in Durres with its kindergarten, primary, secondary or high school—or simply the upper secondary grades.

The first school we visited was an all-girls high school that opened in 1993. Of its 227 students in grades 10 to 12, 190 lived in the dorms. Applicants for admission take an entrance exam, with those highest on the list receiving an acceptance letter. In 2013, 600 applied but only 80 were accepted, with an additional 40 on the wait list. In taking only the highest-performing students, this school—like all others we would vis-it in all countries—has an above-average student body and a very low dropout rate (1-2 percent). Students' test scores determine a comput-er-generated breakdown of the level of scholarship awards given to half of the accepted students. About 8-10 receive a full scholarship, another 8-10 get 80 percent, with similar cohorts in declining percentages. These scholarships are important, because the tuition was the equivalent of $450 a month, compared to $300 at state schools.

The all-boys high school we visited also began in 1993, and almost all students lived in a dormitory. The director spoke proudly of 17 generations of graduates, a total of 800 alumni from 39 countries. All typically continued their studies at a university. Some became diplomats, working in an embassy or in state government. One was the CEO of a hospital and several held directorships in companies or other institutions. This school is near its 200-level capacity, with 177 boys currently enrolled. About 70 percent were on scholarship, based mostly on their academic achievement, although several who were being raised by a single mother also had scholarships. There are six part-time Albanian teachers, and 15 full-time teachers, eight of them Albanians and seven Turkish. The teachers have low incomes and often have a second job, especially if they don't own a home and must pay rent.

The third school we visited was a co-educational K-12 institution in its first year of existence and quartered in an attractive new building. It had 540 students (20 percent male, 80 percent female), with an anticipated enrollment of 700 in the next year (2014-15). Only 20 percent were on scholarship, with three percent of recipients classified as "needy" and orphans. Students in the first grade have seven hours of English classes each week. With 54 staff members, the ratio was one teacher for every 10 students.

One of the administrators at this school would prove to be, as we discovered in subsequent interviews, rather typical of the schools' Turkish leaders in all countries we visited in terms of their previous work experience in other countries. A college graduate in 1997, he spent the next five years teaching in Indonesia before coming to Albania in 2002. After teaching here for four years, he became an administrator at this school, but he confessed to liking teaching better because he could see daily achievements in his students. The Turkish teachers, he explained, get living expenses only but the Albanian teachers earn a salary slightly higher than public school teachers. His teachers visit one-on-one with their students' families, even if they live 5-6 hours away. Each year the teachers also visit 25 cities and towns throughout to give entrance exams to new applicants.

Teachers

In separate private interviews, we sought the outlooks of four Albanian teachers, two women and two men, all of them Muslims. Assured of confidentiality and that nothing would be reported to their administrators, each spoke comfortably and freely to us.

First was a married female high school math teacher, herself a graduate from a Hizmet school. She proved to be the precursor of other Turkish school graduates in expressing her career motivation: "In these [Hizmet] schools we learn how to behave with others, how to make others happy. They gave me something, a wonderful experience, and I must give something back."

She spoke of education in Albania as "a big problem." Why? "The public-school teachers are not prepared well, so the students do not study well." When asked what makes the teachers different here, she replied,

> It is something inside the person. Our impact as a teacher is consistency—keep your word—honesty—reciprocate—language and example—teach character. Also, we always do more extra-curricular activities and take more time to work with them—even join them for parties.

That dedication found voice in another young married woman, an elementary teacher who had two young daughters. In her second year of teaching, her biggest challenge was time management, as her family responsibilities prevented her from preparing her lessons until after nine in the evening, even though she had to get up at five on school days. Besides teaching English, she thought it was important to inculcate in her students the values of "truth, honesty, keep your word and commitments." She didn't lecture on these virtues because "students may already take for granted what parents say, but I lead by example." She admitted, though, to speaking out about diversity, telling her students that they must "never interfere with another person's culture or religion, but instead respect it and them as human beings."

An unmarried biology teacher in his late 30s was a graduate of the state university, but had graduated from a Hizmet high school. That teenage experience inspired him in much the same way as our first interviewee:

I experienced some extra hours of help, discipline, and I learned much from my teachers. Now I see and feel obliged to do the same. It gives me positive energy.

Like our second female interviewee, he also saw himself as a role model:

Students can distinguish between words and behavior. I try to be a positive model to represent good behavior versus bad behavior. Perhaps then, students can become more open-minded, better pre-pared—see the world in a different way—accept different thoughts—be honest.

What he liked most in his work environment was "the discipline, unlike teaching in public schools. Here the teachers are more serious than the majority in public schools—focus is on learning." The teaching, he added, is based on the student:

If he has a problem with studying, it becomes an issue. We (teachers) discuss it. Is it something general or a problem in my class? I try to treat all equally. If someone can't get biology, it's not the end of the world.

An eighth-grade male teacher of Turkish who was in his late twenties was our fourth interviewee. Similarly, he also graduated from the University of Tirana, but had attended a Turkish school before that as a dorm student, attracted to it by advertising leaflets. The first in his family to graduate from college, he was our most enthusiastic subject in talking about the school's mission. Also expressing a desire to pass on to students what had been given to him, he maintained that the school's strongest point was continuity:

Education is a process. A tree cannot be a tree and get fruit without nourishment. It happens over time.

He also liked the fact that school administrators have an open-door policy, that the students can meet with the director, vice director or principal, something virtually unheard of in the public schools. "We are a country in a 45-year transition, a young democracy," he reminded us.

The day will come when Albania changes. Out of the chaos of the 1990s will come self-discipline. Unlike older adults, this generation is learning that you don't need a comrade to control you—you can do it yourself. As we move along a continuum from absolute authority to absolute freedom, we need to find the middle. What we can do is keep our young people away from bad habits. We can show how to bring two people's perspectives together—learn reciprocal respect as a universal value and pass on to students the shared concept of humankind. Not everything in this school is perfect. We have our problems but the school is functioning as an island of hope and promise.

Students

Students constituted the bulk of our interviews. Mostly high school juniors and seniors, their age distributions were five 16-year-olds, ten 17-year-olds, and eight 18-year-olds, for a total of 23 students whom we chose at random. As with their teachers, students were interviewed privately and assured of confidentiality in their replies and of their freedom to avoid answers or to leave at any time. Twelve students lived in an on-site dormitory and the other eleven commuted. Seven students were on full scholarship, four had no scholarship, and the others had partial scholarships ranging from 10 to 80 percent of tuition.

All eight seniors planned to go to college. Three already had acceptances and full scholarships (architecture at Tirana, bioengineering at Berkeley, and engineering at MIT). The others had applied to Albanian, German, and Turkish universities to study architecture, dentistry, medicine, or psychology.

Three students were of the Orthodox faith and reported no problems of any kind with the mostly Muslim student and teacher population. Likewise, the two students who said they were nonreligious (one a declared atheist) said they encountered no pressure or conflict due to their lack of faith. The Muslim students reported no demands regarding the call to prayer, and they often recounted their pleasure in interacting with Christian students. These findings were among our early insights into religion not being part of a hidden curriculum.

One common theme that did emerge was the similarity of opinion about the public schools. Fourteen students interviewed had been in public schools and thus had a personal frame of reference. The other nine students had siblings or friends in public schools and thus offered a secondhand comparison. Again, and again, we heard students say they were in a friendlier and safer environment. They spoke of other contrasts between their school and the public schools: encountering more caring and serious teachers rather than rude, indifferent ones; teachers challenging them intellectually instead of teachers with low expectations; teacher accessibility rather than unavailability after class; fairness in grading, not favoritism due to corruption (bribery); and firm yet friendly discipline versus its absence in the public schools. Typical was the comment of this eleventh-grade boy:

> Teachers in the public school know nothing about you, but here teachers develop relationships, talk to you like friends. Not only for lessons, but they teach you how to be "a man."

When asked what impact they thought their school had on them as persons, another common theme surfaced, one that we found in Bosnia and Herzegovina and would later surface among students in other countries. The expressions varied: "cultural openness," "more open-minded," "not to prejudge others because they are different," "become a better person," "be more accepting," "be more comfortable with people who are different," "appreciate people more beyond the superficial". However, the common denominator was respect and tolerance for the "other."

Alumni

We interviewed three graduates of Mehmet Akif College (Kolegji Mehmet Akif), a male from the boys' school and two females from the girls' school.

The women were both in their late twenties and graduates of the University of Tirana. The first woman, now a teacher, had spent 15 years in Hizmet schools. When asked what she liked about her educational experience, she said there were many things, but especially the liberal viewpoint, how the teachers fired her ambition and taught her good time management. She spoke in glowing terms about how the school promoted positive relations with others, and also how it helped her become more self-reliant and self-confident. The second woman, the product of

14 years in Hizmet schools and part of the business community, spoke to her satisfaction in learning English and going abroad with classmates for cultural exchanges. She also liked the emphasis on truthfulness, respect for others, and a healthy emphasis on pride for one's country.

Learning English and traveling abroad were also valuable take-aways for a male interviewee in his late thirties, who graduated in 1998. Now a company import manager, he had traveled to the United States to experience that culture, and he told us about feeling good that Americans did not judge others by where they are from. He spoke highly of his teachers and the discipline in his secondary school in contrast to its absence in state schools.

Parents

Of the eight parents we interviewed, three were females and five were males, two of the latter of the Orthodox faith, while all others were Muslims. Two of the women were teachers, one of them a department head, and the third worked with her husband in their export business. Among the four other fathers were two businessmen, a journalist, and a Supreme Court judge. Seven of the eight parents held bachelor or advanced degrees. The furniture designer who did not was married to a woman who was a teacher with a master's degree. Given the previously mentioned fact that most Albanians have a tenth-grade education, these parents clearly represented an educational elite segment of the population.

Upon inquiry, we learned our random selection of parents resulted in this skewed distribution in the educational background of parents occurred because other parents were either working or else lived some distance from the schools. Indeed, school buses not only provided the means of access for many families, but also offered peace-of-mind safety through door-to-door pickup and return that made the school even more appealing.

Several common themes emerged from the parents' comments, regardless of their religion, background, or which of the three schools their children attended. All knew the schools by reputation for their academic quality, and they were lavish in their praise of the teachers for their dedication, competency, and pro-student friendliness. These elements were especially important, they suggested, for a country that has been a democracy for only 20 years after decades of a dictatorship. "Our society will benefit from informed new leaders," said one father, and a mother suggested, "These children will make this world better and their businesses better." Another father said that he already saw evidence of change in the quality and empathetic care from young hospital doctors treating his mother's illness.

Compassion, in fact, was a recurrent strand in the parents' remarks. Despite the exclusive nature of these schools with their strict entrance requirements and tuition costs, several parents insisted their children were not isolated or "on an island with a disconnect with those raised with nothing," as one said. "Here they learn acceptance and tolerance of other cultures," said a Muslim father. An Orthodox mother spoke positively about the character building her daughter was experiencing and more: "She is learning to communicate, to build bridges with other communities, to give value to it and help others. This is so important today."

Another Muslim father stated,

> This school plays an important role in empathy building. When there was an explosion disaster not too long ago, they asked the students to raise money to help with a food fair and other activities. The children learned about the pleasure in giving.

Not only were their children becoming well prepared for the future, but also, they felt that they were developing good work habits. For those going to another country to further their education, they believed that this would be an important factor for their self-reliance. "My daughter will be alone in the United States studying economics [at Brown]," said an Orthodox father." She will go there knowing how to best organize her time, make friends, and succeed." A Muslim mother felt equally competent: "It will be easier for my daughter to study abroad because of this school," she offered, "because she learned other languages and interacted with other cultures." Their children's ease of interrelating with those of different cultures was mentioned repeatedly.

The *in loco parentis* responsibility of educators – a doctrine that is rooted in British and American common law traditions (Lee 2011) – emerged as another affirmative component in parents' favorable attitudes. "I am very busy with my own business," said an Orthodox father, "but with the school bus and this school, I know she is in safe hands." A

Muslim father also favored the school's supplementing his childrearing activities:

> I have been paying tuition for eight years, but I am willing to make the sacrifice to this five-star school. I don't have much time to look after my kids [ninth-grade girl and third-grade boy], but the school does this for me, including taking them on vacation in the summer school. We do maybe 30 percent of teaching values and the school does 70 percent—things like how time is spent, be responsible, not aggressive but calm—ambitious—independent—ensure you do nothing wrong.

Another Muslim father with two children in the school (15-year-old son and 13-year-old daughter] expressed his satisfaction in the emphasis on 1) integrity, 2) telling the truth no matter how difficult, 3) how to relate to others, and 4) being charitable as "some of the best things done at the school besides the academic instruction."

The Universities

We visited two Gülen-inspired universities in Tirana. Both were fairly new universities and rapidly expanding. Nationally accredited and linked to other universities in exchange programs, they can be positively compared to public universities in terms of staff qualifications, facilities, and curricula offerings.

Epoka University

Launched in 2007, Epoka University was the older of the two universities we visited, and it received accreditation in 2012 from the Albanian Ministry of Education and Science, the same year that the University moved to a brand-new campus near Rinas Airport, just outside the capital city of Tirana. Each year its enrollments have been increasing, now exceeding 1,400 students, including more than 300 graduate students.

The Faculty of Economics and Administrative Sciences has Departments of Economics, Banking and Finance, Business Administration and Political Science and International Relations. Within the Faculty of Architecture and Engineering are the Departments of Architecture, Civil Engineering and Computer Engineering. Degree programs include ten at the bachelor's level, eight Master of Science degrees, nine Professional

Master's degrees, and six Ph.D. programs are in the fields of architecture, business administration, civil engineering, computer engineering, economics, and international relations. Except for the Bachelor in Banking and Finance program taught in Albanian, all other study programs are in English. The University also has four research centers: the Center for European Studies (CES), the Center of Research and Design in Applied Sciences (CORDA), the Yunus Center for Social Business and Sustainability (YCSBS), and the Continuous Education Center (CEC).

A Gülen-inspired secular school like the Albanian feeder schools we visited, the University attracts students from Azerbaijan, Kosovo, North Macedonia, Montenegro, and Turkey. Its modern facilities are aesthetically appealing, and fully loaded with all of the latest fiber-optic technological equipment. Host to one or two international conferences each year, the co-educational university is integrated into the European Union through its student exchange program (Erasmus).

Bedër University

Begun in 2011 by the Muslim Community of Albania but operated by the Sema Foundation, Bedër University was a natural extension of the opening of the madrasas twenty years earlier. On our visit, administrators downplayed their institution as an "Islamic university" as some have called it. Although it does have a Department of Islamic Studies, it also has six other departments: Communication Sciences, Education Sciences, English Language and Literature, Law, and Turkish Language and Literature.

On our visit, we found that the university functioned in a seven-story suburban office building, but faculty and administrators were looking forward to their relocation in 2015 to a new campus. By the time the final construction phase ended in 2017, it quadrupled student enrollment from its then-total of about 500 undergraduate and graduate students to the current total of 2,000 from 15 countries (Edarabia 2020).

Two-thirds of its staff were Albanians; most of the rest were Turkish, although a scattering of six other countries were represented, including three from the United States and one from the United Kingdom. Women constituted one-third of the faculty. Forty faculty members had a Ph.D. and another twenty-six were Ph.D. candidates. An additional twenty-five held a master's degree.

Facilities—classrooms, offices, computer and language labs, auditoriums and conference halls, library and dining hall—were equipped with state-of-the-art technology and aesthetically pleasing. Though small in size compared to its Albanian counterparts, Bedër University appeared to be academically sound and with excellent potential.

Retrospect

As in Bosnia and Herzegovina, an impressive number of positive comments were made by the interviewee cohorts in the facilities we visited. Not surprisingly, religion was far less a factor in self-identity here. At the primary and secondary levels, the issues of discipline, safety, quality teaching, and student-faculty rapport—in stark contrast to what respondents said existed in the public schools—were highly important features of the Albanian Hizmet schools that prompted the favorable remarks we heard over and over.

In November 2020, several of the Gülen-inspired schools in Albania experienced police raids without a warrant or court order. The police confiscated tax invoices, sales ledgers, student registers, and contracts with parents and students. No irregularities were found, but this increased government pressure came after Turkish government efforts to close these schools as part of its foreign policy (*Turkish Minute* 2020).

References

"Albania." 2020. *CIA World Factbook*. Retrieved March 1, 2021 (https://www.cia. gov/library/publications/the-world-factbook/geos/al.html).

"Beder University." 2020. Edarabia. Retrieved March 1, 2021 (https://www.edarabia.com/beder-universty-tirana-albania/).

Çela, Alba, Geron Kamberi, and Elena Pici. 2015. *Albanian Youth 2015*. Tirana, Albania: Friedrich Ebert Foundation.

Cihan News Agency, 2015. "Albanian Speaker Visits Turkish School after Erdoğan Calls for Its Closure." Retrieved March 1, 2021 (https://www.cihan.com.tr/en/albanian-speaker-visits-turkish-school-after-erdogan-calls-for-its-closure-1788401.htm).

Delavande, Adeline and Basit Zafar. 2015. "Stereotypes and Madrasas: Experimental Evidence from Pakistan." *Journal of Economic Behavior & Organization* 118 (October): 247-267.

Education Policy and Data Center. 2020. "Albania." Retrieved March 1, 2021 (http://www.epdc.org/country/albania.html).

Gallup Global Reports, "Religiosity Highest in World's Poorest Nations." Retrieved March 1, 2021 (http://www.gallup.com/poll/142727/religiosity-highest-world-poorest-nations. aspx#2).

Moorey, Chris. 2015. *God Among the Bunkers: The Orthodox Church in Albania Under Enver Hoxha.* Charleston, SC: CreateSpace.

Myriam, Cherti, and Bradley Laura. 2011. *Inside Madrasas: Understanding and Engaging with British-Muslim Faith Supplementary Schools.* London: Institute for Public Policy Research. Retrieved March 1, 2021 (https://www.ippr.org/files/images/media/files/publication/ 2011/11/ inside-madrassas_ Nov2011_8301.pdf).

Öktem, Kerem. 2010. "New Islamic Actors after the Wahhabi Intermezzo: Turkey's Return to the Muslim Balkans." European Studies Centre, University of Oxford.

Organisation for Economic Co-operation and Development (OECD). 2020. OECD Reviews of Evaluation and Assessment in Education: Albania. Paris: OECD Publishing.

Pew Research, Religion & Public Life Project. 2012. "The World's Muslims: Unity and Diversity." Retrieved March 1, 2021 (http://www.pewforum.org/2012/08/09/the-worlds-muslims-unity-and-diversity-2-religious-commitment/).

Turkish Minute. 2020. "Formerly Gülen-Linked Schools in Albania Face Growing Gov't Pressure." Retrieved March 1, 2021 (https://hizmet-news.com/25361/formerly-gulen-linked-schools-in-albania-face-growing-govt-pressure/#.X8-s69hKiUk).

4

KAZAKHSTAN

Kazakhstan, located in Central Asia, is the world's largest land-locked country and the ninth largest country in the world. One remnant of the old Persian Empire in this region is in the country's name and that of its neighbors (Tajikistan, Uzbekistan, Kyrgyzstan, and Turkmenistan). In Farsi, the language of present-day Iran and the ancient Persian Empire, the suffix -stan means "land" or "place of." Kazakhstan is thus the land of the Kazakhs, whose ancestry is a mix of Turkic and Mongol nomadic tribes.

Under Russian domination for about two centuries, Kazakhstan became a Soviet Republic in 1925. Soviet repression, together with a program of forced agricultural collectivization in the 1930s, led to great suffering and a massive number of deaths. Persistent food shortages in Russia led Nikita Khrushchev in the 1950s to launch a successful "Virgin Lands Campaign" to induce Russian farmers to migrate to the steppe land in northern Kazakhstan for grain cultivation. Successive years of bountiful harvest (until soil depletion and erosion a decade later) led to an immense influx of settlers (mostly ethnic Russians, but also other nationalities, particularly Volga Germans). By the time Kazakhstan became an independent nation in 1991, ethnic Kazakhs were a minority.

Beginning in the mid-1990s though, that population composition changed. Over the next ten years, hundreds of thousands of non-Muslim ethnic minorities left, particularly Slavs and Germans. In seeking to build a new nation with a strong identity, the national government initiated a repatriation program to induce the return of a million ethnic Kazakhs, particularly from the neighboring Xinjiang region of China, and also Mongolia, Tajikistan, and Uzbekistan. As a consequence, the Kazakhs again became the majority in their own land, and they now constitute more than two-thirds of the total population.

Societal Overview

Of the three countries with large Muslim populations covered in this study, Kazakhstan—about four times the size of Texas—has the largest population (19 million) and a high percentage of Muslims (70 percent). Another 26 percent are Christian (90 percent of them Russian Orthodox), and the remainder are mostly atheists and unspecified others. As mentioned, the largest ethnic group is the Kazakhs (68 percent), followed by Russians (19 percent), Uzbeks (3 percent), Uighurs and Ukrainians (1.5 percent), Tatars and Germans at 1 percent (CIA World Factbook 2020).

Kazakhstan also exhibits some of the lowest levels of religiosity among Muslim countries. Only four percent say they pray several times daily, and just two percent perform *salat* (the five prayers daily that constitute the second pillar of Islam). When asked, 18 percent said religion is "very important" in their lives—half that in Bosnia and Herzegovina, and slightly higher than in Albania (Pew Research 2012).

Kazakhstan's economy is the largest of the Central Asian states, mainly due to the country's vast natural resources (major deposits of petroleum, natural gas, coal, manganese, iron and chrome ore, cobalt, copper, lead, nickel, zinc, bauxite, gold, and uranium). It also has a large agricultural sector (livestock and grain), but has begun to diversify its economy into such areas as pharmaceuticals, telecommunications, and food processing. Its literacy rate is nearly 100 percent, with an average 15-year educational level among the populace (*CIA World Factbook* 2020).

The country contains a vast steppe (flat land without trees except those near lakes and rivers), extending from the Volga River in the west to the Altai Mountains in the east –and the plains of Western Siberia in the north to the oases and deserts of Central Asia in the south. Winters can be notoriously harsh in the northern part of the country.

Schools

Almaty is the country's largest city (population 1.9 million) and the former capital until 1997. It lies in the mountainous southeastern part of the country, a few thousand feet above sea level, and its mountains provide a spectacular natural backdrop against the manmade skyscrapers, as well as a seductive lure for hiking and skiing enthusiasts. A mixture of old and new buildings—with the latter including glitzy shopping malls, expensive high-rise apartments, coffee lounges, fancy restaurants, and dance-till-dawn nightclubs—Almaty is a cosmopolitan blend of East European, Russian, and Kazakh influences.

In this city we first visited an all-girls secondary school, grades seven to eleven, that began in 1993 and had produced more than 800 graduates, almost all of whom went on to further schooling. Of the 320 current enrollees, about half were resident students living in dorms. About 90 percent were Kazakhs, and the remainder of the population consists of ten other nationalities, especially Germans, Russians, Tatars, Koreans, and Iranians.

Like other schools we visited previously, a highly judicious process, based on entrance test scores, winnows the number of acceptances. At the time of our visit, the newest class of 45 students emerged from a field of 550 applicants. The selectivity extends to the school itself. We learned that out of 9,000 schools in the country, this one was ranked in the top ten by the Kazakhstan Ministry of Education and Science.

Next on our visit was an all-boys secondary school. Although part of the Hizmet school system, it is nonetheless a state school, and so it provides very few full scholarships (about 30). About 250 or its 400 students commute and the rest live in dorms. These students also are from the top echelon of entrance exam takers. The newest class of 110 students came out of a total of 1,300 applicants. Twelve of the 35 teachers at this school were Kazakhs.

Our third "college" (secondary school) was co-educational but only in the second year of operation. It had 340 students, 100 of them living in dorms. Five of its 23 teachers were Turkish, as was its first and only principal, who had previously served as principal for seven years at another school in Astana. From him we got a better sense of what it costs a family to send a child to a school where only 4-5 students receive partial "scholarships of need." Tuition was the equivalent of $2,000 USD and board is the same amount. In a country where an average worker earns less than $500 USD monthly, that is a considerable amount spent on education (Trading Economics 2020).

The other major urban center is the new capital city of Astana (renamed Nur-Sultan in 2019). Not even in existence as a city until 1997, it is now the second largest city in Kazakhstan. Situated in the northern part of the country, its temperature extremes range from highs in the mid-nineties Fahrenheit in summer to as low as forty degrees below zero in winter. Weather extremes, however, do not affect the spectacular Khan Shatyr Entertainment Center. Sunlight shines through its transparent tent covering, and a special chemical lining protects those inside from the brutal icy winter and helps maintain its special microclimate, aided by an efficient heating and cooling system. This impressive tent structure, which changes colors at night and streams in natural light during the day, is 490 feet tall and covers an area larger than 10 football stadiums. It includes a shopping center with many shops, squares and cobbled streets, a boating river, and an indoor beach, with sand imported from the Maldives. Elsewhere in this city situated on the flat land of the steppes are many other unique futuristic skyscrapers, as well as the highly prominent 328-foot Baiterek tower, giving the city a science-fiction skyline.

In Astana, we visited an all-boys high school, begun in 1994 and with a current enrollment of 350 students. The principal, an English teacher for eight years and then in his first year as principal, told us that five of the 25 teachers (19 male and six female) were Turkish. Once again, the elite nature of the student body was obvious in only 50 students accepted that semester out of 1,300 applicants.

Teachers

As in the Balkan countries we visited, the teachers we randomly interviewed in Kazakhstan also exhibited enthusiasm, dedication, high morale and commitment to the twin goals of providing quality instruction and inspiration to their students. Typical was this comment of a Kazakh male, an eleventh-grade English teacher in his sixth year of teaching. A graduate of the very school in which he was now teaching, he commented:

> The mission of a teacher is to teach the subject and values, be a role model. Each person is going to become a part of society, and so each must contribute to society. For me, it is shared energy, giving back a little of what you've been given.

As idealistic as we found these teachers, they also appeared to us to be rooted in realistic self-assessments. Perhaps this attitude was best expressed by another male teacher, a Russian married to a Kazakh woman, both of them with advanced degrees:

> We're not perfect. We are human beings with faults like everyone else, and sometimes we fail. But the important thing is that we try for our students, and our focus is clear.

A married Kazakh female biology teacher, graduate of a public university and with nine years of teaching experience, spoke of her high job satisfaction in working with such highly motivated students. She liked getting closer to her students beyond the formal confines of the classroom so that she not only "conveyed class lessons but also life lessons, which are just as important."

A married female English teacher also liked that "the students want to learn." She declared:

> Teachers are peacemakers, not troublemakers. The students see our behavior and hopefully model their behavior after ours. It is character education. People have to help other people. Even if only a minority of them takes these values, it's a good thing.

This woman, in her sixth year of teaching, also provided insight in the staff's proactive steps in their teaching their students living in the dorms:

> In the beginning we have an organization meeting with the parents. We listen to what they want and they approve our topics. Then, during the school year, the teachers meet every Friday. We discuss how the students are doing and we share our knowledge. We call the parents and talk to them about everything.

In loco parentis apparently exists in a more comprehensive form in Hizmet educational institutions, and even more so among those living on school grounds day and night, week after week.

Students

In Almaty and Astana, we interviewed 36 students, 21 females and 15 males. All but three were Muslims, but not one female— wore the hijab, much like other women in Kazakhstan. Among our mostly Kazakh student interviewees also were nine Korean, Russian, Tatar Turkish, or Uzbek students. They were ages fifteen (three), sixteen (seven), seventeen (eighteen), eighteen (six), and two graduates were in their twenties.

Common threads we had discerned in last year's student interviews in Bosnia-Herzegovina and Albania emerged also among the Kazakh students. In response to what they liked most about their school, students overwhelmingly mentioned their teachers, often making comparisons with experiences with public school teachers that they, friends or siblings had had. "They are good people, with great hearts," said one Kazakh student. "In the public schools, teachers are rude and some even try to be. I'm happier here." In fact, it was rare to encounter a student who failed to mention teachers in positive terms. Of particular interest were remarks from the non-Muslim students. For example, a 16-year-old Kazakh Catholic boy told us, "I like the kind of people our teachers are. They are, like, perfect to me. They're professional, always dressed up. They're not our friends as much as they are like our brothers." A non-religious Russian girl who was seventeen put it this way: "I like the atmosphere. Our teachers are very friendly and warm. We can talk to them because they are interested in us and in our work."

Students who had previously attended public schools remarked on what they considered major distinctions. A 15-year-old Uzbek girl liked the differences: "I feel at home here. The teachers are friendly, always smiling, and they understand us better than teachers in the public schools." A 16-year-old Kazakh Muslim girl offered, "I like the teacher relationships. They're closer than in other schools. They are kind and helpful." Besides attesting to friendliness and a near-kinship bond with their teachers, the students also frequently used such descriptors as "helping," "caring," "encouraging," and "sharing."

We also sought to gauge the school's impact on student values and character development, particularly among seniors because they had completed an extended period of schooling and were perhaps the most affected by these Gülen-inspired high schools. Through a series of questions in that area, we detected two commonalities. The first paralleled previous student comments about increased tolerance and empathy for unlike others, fulfilling one component of the Hizmet schools' mission statement. An 18-year-old Kazakh male provided this self-analysis: "Openness, respect for other ideas, tolerance, and generosity are the most important values I have learned from my teachers and tutors at the Turkish school."

Another 18-year-old Kazakh male saw changes in himself that were due to his experiences in school: "Before, I just lived my life. I didn't think about things, but here they push you. They changed my way of thinking about three things: study, friendship, look for good in people." A 17-year-old Kazakh young woman disclosed her attitudinal shifts: "Now I have friends who are Turkish and Azerbaijani. When I first met them, they looked different and I thought they were, but I learned they were not."

Gülen's call for interfaith and intercultural dialogue no doubt inspires his followers in the Hizmet schools to spread that message through conversation and example and thereby promote greater social acceptance of other racial and ethnic groups. However, "learning by doing," has long been recognized by educators as one of the best means of mastering material, and this concept of experiential education can extend to the shaping of attitudes (Roberts 2012).

By itself, diversity in the classroom does not ensure greater social acceptance of the "other." Social isolation, indifference, or the formation of inwardly turned cliques, for instance, could work against any positive attitudinal adjustment. However, if social interaction occurs among members of diverse groups with equal status, it will more likely moderate one's views of the "other," an argument advanced by proponents of the intergroup contact hypothesis (Pettigrew and Tropp 2005).

In the Hizmet schools, the teachers are proactive in forming mixed groups for class presentations and/or projects, in order to accomplish more than students mastering some increment of knowledge. This arrangement gives evidence of effectiveness. To illustrate, a 16-year-old Tatar girl related, "I appreciate now other people's perspectives. I was more selfish before, but now we study together and I see we're all equal."

From a minority standpoint, cooperative group projects can provide a mechanism through which hesitancy due to self-consciousness and a lack of self-confidence can be overcome. A 16-year-old Korean boy gave supportive testimony in saying, "As a minority here, I learned to communicate and speak freely. We became close to each other, a brotherhood." Of course, this teaching technique can help shy students of any nationality. A 17-year-old Kazakh male, for instance, said, "Here we have mixed nationalities, and by working with them, I improved my self-confidence with others, because they stressed teamwork. Now I have social skills for the future."

The second component was particularly heartening, partly because Americans come from a society increasingly striving for greater gender equality, and partly because of a belief shared among many people about the supposed subservience of Muslim women. Here in Kazakhstan, the unsolicited remarks by numerous and poised young females (some of which are shared below), were similar to those of the young women interviewed in both Albania and Bosnia-Herzegovina. What could have been interpreted simply as individual personality characteristics under more limited investigation, now appeared to be the result of a successful education effort that was intertwined within the hidden curriculum of achieving self-fulfillment, irrespective of gender or external social forces because of the cultural milieu of these schools.

Many experts believe that shyness is biologically rooted, but also considerable agreement exists that, additionally, socialization plays a role in shaping its development. Further, culture—instilled in parents' and educators' beliefs, values, and expectations—shape individual experiences and personality (Blakemore and Hill 2008; Brinkman et al. 2014; Crozier 2000). Traditional gender role socialization usually swayed girls away from science and math classes (Berg 2009), but in these schools in Kazakhstan we found examples comparable to the previous two countries visited of a gender-equal learning environment that encouraged full potential of both boys and girls. For example, a 16-year-old Kazakh girl related, "I was shy when I first arrived at this school, but now I am more open and talkative. I have built up my self-confidence." Similarly, an 18-year-old Kazakh female said, "I've grown in self-confidence as school broadened my mind, and I became able to have good friends who are Ukrainian and Turkish." These are representative comments. In a noncompetitive environment where different points of view are encouraged, along with an emphasis on cooperative learning and helping one another whenever needs arise, formerly timid or reserved females—by their own self-descriptions—grow into adulthood unrestrained by sexist stereotypes.

Alumni

Two Kazakh women were visiting their high school alma mater on the day we visited one of the schools and we seized the opportunity to interview them. Now graduates of the state university, both had spent most of their childhood and teenage years in Hizmet schools. Asked to reflect upon all that schooling, we inquired as to how they thought that education had shaped them. From one woman we heard further testimony to the previous point about Hizmet educators fostering female empowerment:

> I liked their liberal viewpoint. They taught me, as a woman, to be self-reliant and self-confident. They fired my ambition, as well as teaching me good time management and how to relate to others.

The second woman agreed that she became a stronger person and developed the self-assurance to travel abroad and learn more about other cultures. She added, "I also became a better person, more truthful and patriotic, and learned to respect older people more."

Parents

All the parents we interviewed were Kazakhs. Some held advanced degrees and were in professional careers; others were blue-collar workers. A farmer spoke to us of his pleasure that the school also taught the Kazakh language and culture, so the children could relearn the cultural traditions which the government, under Soviet domination until 1991, tried to "strip away."

Although Kazakh public schools did not suffer as notorious a reputation as in those Albania and Bosnia-Herzegovina, parents nevertheless saw important distinctions in the Hizmet schools. Often, we heard comments about the excellence of the schools as exemplified by the comments of this father, a petroleum engineer: "The quality of education in this school is unequaled, and they teach in English, so necessary in this global economy."

Parents also found their children's teachers just as dedicated as the Albanian and Bosnian parents. As one Kazakh father said, "These teachers are more educated and polite, and they are multilingual." That last point found different forms of expression from many parents who thought the public schools too limited in their world view. This mother's comment illustrates such thinking:

> Our children need to live in an interconnected world where they must be able to appreciate cultural differences.

Parental awareness of the intercultural school environment, both in social interactions and in advocacy of intergroup fellowship, often arose in the interviews, as typified by this father's comments when asked if he noted any changes in his daughter since enrolling in the school:

> My daughter no longer fights people and, for the first time, she has good friends who are not our people.

Positive feedback about the teachers was perhaps the most common aspect of these interviews with parents. A mother told us, "Teachers here generously share their talents and knowledge in engaging with the students." A father expressed great satisfaction in telling us:

> This is an altruistic environment. Everyone gives; no one takes. The teachers sacrifice themselves for the children. You can trust these people, believe me.

Financial Supporters

One evening in Almaty we visited with a Turkish expatriate, an affluent entrepreneur who ran several successful business ventures. He lived in a spacious apartment on an upper floor in a new high-rise building. After a delicious home-cooked dinner, we engaged in a long, pleasant conversation on many subjects. Of particular interest to us, of course, was to hear his motivation for financially supporting the Hizmet schools in this city. His charitable contributions went beyond *zakat* (the third pillar of Islam of giving support to the needy), and we wanted to learn to what extent his thinking paralleled the financial supporters we interviewed last year. It turned out his reasons for donating also centered on the two main missions of the schools: quality education and intercultural understanding. He put it this way:

> Too many people use money for bad things. Good people must use money for good things. What could be better than having as many

schools as possible that provide the best education and positive views about people?

As with so many other Turkish businessmen supporters whom we would interview, this man's Islamic faith and humanitarian values were the driving factors to give generously of his income in support of these schools. No named scholarships or buildings or building wings were concomitant with major donations. In fact, in Islam true charitable donations are those for which the giver should not seek any ego gratification:

> God, in His boundless mercy, promises rewards for helping those in need with one basic condition that zakat be paid in the name of God; one should not expect or demand any worldly gains from the beneficiaries nor aim at making one's name as a philanthropist. The feelings of a beneficiary should not be hurt by making him feel inferior or reminding him of the assistance (Mufti 2019).

Nazarbayev University

Although it is a state university and thus not part of our study, as academics we must mention the impressive sight of Nazarbayev University, an autonomous research university founded in 2010 and with a current undergraduate enrollment of about 3,000, with about 1,600 master's and doctoral students. Its male-female ratio is fairly even, and it is clearly a state-of-the-art campus. However, what awes the first-time visitor is the university's mega structure that covers 25 acres, almost three times the size of the Houston Astrodome. You enter into a massive courtyard atrium with a soaring roof, and see dozens of palm trees, several fountains and pools surrounded by beautifully landscaped plants. How incongruous those palm trees must be in the dead of the typical bitterly cold winters! Four massive wings off each side of this architectural centerpiece house various schools, and at the end is the School of Humanities and Social Sciences. Enclosed skywalks or corridors connect all other buildings: research laboratories, several auditoriums, two student dormitory buildings (616 rooms), different sized auditoriums, two university staff residential buildings (260 units), and a sports center with a swimming pool, its water heated by solar energy.

Retrospect

Comments by our various Kazakh respondents about the Hizmet schools revealed commonalities with those in the other Muslim-majority countries previously visited: Bosnia-Herzegovina and Albania. However, Kazakhstan's history and culture did influence behavior, perceptions, and functioning. For example, wearing the hijab has never been part of Kazakh culture, and the absence of females wearing it the schools was readily apparent. In Bosnia and Herzegovina, we often saw many girls and women without a head covering, but at the same time it was not uncommon to see others with the *hijab* as well. In contrast, we encountered virtually no girl or woman wearing one, not in the schools, public places, or homes we visited.

These schools also reflected the government's efforts at state-building and ethnic identification since its independence in 1991 (Beacháin and Kevlihan 2011). One such effort of President Nursultan Nazarbayev has been to eliminate the use of the Russian language in favor of the Kazakh language in the schools, government, and everyday life. Unique, therefore, in the Kazakh Hizmet schools is the inclusion of Kazakh language courses, a feature highly appreciated by the parents to whom we spoke.

References

Beacháin, Donnacha Ó, and Rob Kevlihan. 2011. "State-building, Identity, and Nationalism in Kazakhstan: Some Preliminary Thoughts." Working Papers in International Studies. Center for International Studies, Dublin City University. Retrieved March 1, 2021 (https://www.academia.edu/2054132/State_building_identity_and_nationalism_in_Kazakhstan_some_preliminary_thoughts).

Berg, Christine. 2009. *Gender Socialization: Why Do Girls Stop Taking Science and Math Classes?* Saarbrücken, Germany: VDM Publishing.

Blakemore, Judith E. Owen and Craig A. Hill, "The Child Gender Socialization Scale: A Measure to Compare Traditional and Feminist Parents," *Sex Roles* 58 (2008): 192–207.

Brinkman, Britney G., Kelly Rabenstein, Lee A Rosén, and Toni Zimmerman, "Children's Gender Identity Development: The Dynamic

Negotiation Process Between Conformity and Authenticity," *Youth & Society* 46:6 (November 2014): 835–852.

Chen, Xinyin. 2019. "Culture and Shyness in Childhood and Adolescence." *New Ideas in Psychology* 53: 58-66.

Crozier, W. Ray, ed. 2000. *Shyness: Development, Consolidation and Change.* New York: Routledge.

"Kazakhstan." 2020. *CIA World Factbook.* Retrieved March 1, 2021 (https://www.cia.gov/library/publications/the-world-factbook/geos/kz.html).

Kenway, Jane and Sue Willis. 1998. *Answering Back: Girls, Boys, and Feminism in Schools.* New York: Routledge.

Lee, Philip. 2011. "The Curious Life of In Loco Parentis at American Universities." *Higher Education in Review* 8: 65-90

Marks, Jaime L., Chun Bun Lam, and Susan M. McHale, "Family Patterns of Gender Role Attitudes," *Sex Roles* 61 (2009): 221–234.

Mufti, Imam. 2019. "The Third Pillar of Islam: Compulsory Charity." Retrieved March 1, 2021 (https://www.islamreligion.com/articles/46/third-pillar-of-islam/).

Pettigrew, Thomas F., and Linda E. Tropp, "Allport's Intergroup Contact Hypothesis: Its History and Influence," pp. 262-277, in John F. Davidio, Peter Glick, and Laurie Rudman (eds.), *On the Nature of Prejudice: Fifty Years After Allport* (New York: Wiley-Blackwell, 2005).

Pew Research, Religion & Public Life Project. 2012. "The World's Muslims: Unity and Diversity." Retrieved March 1, 2021 (http://www.pewforum.org/2012/08/09/the-worlds-muslims-unity-and-diversity-2-religious-commitment/).

Roberts, Jay E. 2012. *Beyond Learning by Doing: Theoretical Currents in Experiential Education* (New York: Routledge).

Trading Economics. "Kazakhstan Minimum Monthly Wage: 2000-2019 Data." Retrieved March 1, 2021 (https://tradingeconomics.com/kazakhstan/wages).

5

ROMANIA

Like the aforementioned three countries we visited in 2012 and 2013, Romania also was under communist domination for about half a century. However, unlike the others, Muslims are a small minority, constituting only about one percent of the population. This is a Christian country of more than 21 million, with nine in ten people identifying as such. Thus, the similarity of political histories but the differences in religious affiliations made Romania an ideal choice in making cross-cultural comparisons of Hizmet schools.

Located in southeastern Europe, and bordering the Black Sea, Romania is about twice the size of Pennsylvania, and just slightly smaller than Oregon. The country shares borders with Bulgaria and Serbia, that southern boundary mostly formed by the Danube River. Hungary to the northwest and Moldova and the Ukraine to the north are also its neighbors. The Carpathian Mountains—the third longest mountain range in Europe—dominate the central part of the country.

Democracy was a long time coming to Romania—from kings to Soviet occupation to the decades-long rule of dictator Nicolae Ceausescu, who took power in 1965 and was overthrown and executed in 1989. During his extremely brutal reign, he enacted his Francophile views by coldheartedly displacing 40,000 people and razing a four-square-mile part of the center city to build wide boulevards patterned after those in Paris. Even more extravagant is the massive Palace of Parliament, one of the world's largest and by far most expensive administration buildings. Home to its two legislative branches and three museums, and containing eight underground levels including a large nuclear bunker at the bottom, it remains about 70 percent empty (Malathronas 2014).

Societal Overview

From an ethnic standpoint, Romania is fairly homogeneous, with more than 83 percent of the population identifying as Romanian (*CIA World Factbook* 2020). The Romani (Gypsies) are only about three percent but are a rather visible minority with slightly darker complexions, clothing, and ornately decorated houses. Germans and Ukrainians are small minorities, and Hungarians constitute the largest minority group (six percent), and they strongly seek to maintain their national identity. To illustrate, during a two-week lecture tour in 2006 under the auspices of U.S. State Department's international exchange program, this author conferred with the Hungarian members of the Romanian Parliament. They were adamant in asserting their national identity as "Romanian Hungarians," not "Hungarian Romanians," even though native-born. In a part of the world where bloodlines are more important than birthplace, they did not see *Romanian* as the common denominator like Americans (e.g., "Irish American" or "Mexican American"). As such, they and other Romanian Hungarians promote their own language and have schools with instruction in Hungarian. Would such thinking have an impact on a Hizmet school's mission to promote acceptance and interaction with other cultures?

Unlike its Slovak neighbors, the Romanian language is Latin based, a legacy from centuries earlier when the Roman Empire occupied the area. Romania is a secular state and has no national religion even though 89 percent follow Eastern Orthodox teachings. Another six percent are Protestant, and four percent are Roman Catholic (*CIA World Factbook* 2020). Although just one percent are Muslims, Islam has been a presence for 700 years, and their history in Romania has been one of peaceful coexistence.

According to the Pew Research Center, Romania is the most religious of 34 European countries. Among adults, 55 percent described themselves as "highly religious," and half said they attended worship services at least monthly, while 44 percent said they pray daily (Pew Research Center 2018). In addition, 64 percent responded that they believed in God with absolute certainty.

The population is rather evenly distributed across the country, which is not as urbanized as its neighbors (UN Population Division 2018). The largest city is its capital, Bucharest, with a population of about 1.8 million, and that is the location of the K-12 Hizmet school complex that we visited.

Schools

In our visit with the General Director of the Liceul international schools, we learned that the first school was established in 1994 in Costanța, the oldest continuously inhabited city in Romania. Founded by the Romans around 600 B.C.E., it is situated in the eastern part of the country on the Black Sea. Costanța was a logical choice for the first Hizmet school in Romania because Muslims, as just mentioned, lived in peaceful coexistence there for 700 years. By the time of our visit in 2014, 11 such schools were operating throughout the country, with a total enrollment of about 3,300 students. About 80 percent were Romanians, and the remaining students were from several dozen other countries, slightly more than half from Turkey. About one-fifth of the 400 teachers were Turkish, and the rest were Romanians.

Our interviews took place at a middle school (grades five through eight) and a high school in Bucharest. Combined here were 638 students, 100 of them Muslims, of whom 52 were Turks. All were commuting students. Only six teachers among the 86 were Turkish, with the remainder all Romanian. Although the curriculum is basically the same as in the public schools, the schools' reputations rest on their emphasis on math, physics, chemistry, and biology. They have amassed dozens of medals in the inter-school Olympiad academic competitions that are an integral part of Hizmet schools everywhere.

The schools' director had extensive educational experience in other Hizmet schools: 11 years in Moldova and four years in Indonesia. He was in his fourth year at this Bucharest school, and his enthusiasm for his work had not waned. "To feel that you help someone, you cannot describe it," was how he summed up his life's work.

Teachers and Staff

A Turkish female chemistry teacher with an M.S. degree and ten years teaching experience spoke about her all-inclusive role as both instructor and counselor:

> We are a piece of the puzzle. We do care about our students as persons and give them extra help when they need it. Young people sometimes get into arguments with each other, so we try to calm them down and negotiate a solution acceptable to both sides.

A foreign languages teacher, with degrees from the University of Bucharest and a Spanish university, answered a newspaper ad and now is in a Hizmet school for the first time. She finds the contrast refreshing:

> In the state schools there is a rigid curriculum and style. Here we have an international environment where teachers have more contact with students. The emphasis is on motivation, so you can use flexibility in methodology. You have freedom to choose, and use a cooperative, informal approach instead of a formal one.

Other teachers we interviewed each displayed a dedicated professionalism, but it was more than these educators attempting to impress outsiders. Seeping through their conversations were joy and satisfaction in what they were doing. From what we discerned, the positive work environment and their internalized sense of purpose propelled them beyond seeing their responsibilities solely as completing lesson plans.

We also spoke to the woman in charge of school admissions, a graduate of Romanian state schools, and with experience in the public schools in England. In addition to contrasting the state and Hizmet Romanian schools (much larger class sizes and less emphasis on conceptual learning in the former), she addressed how they maintain a protective school environment:

> One-fourth of our students are bused here from their homes and back again, and parents are happy with their safety, both in traveling and once they are here. Through persuasion and activism, we discourage bullying. When it happens, we attempt conflict resolution and, if necessary, talk to the parents.

Students

Interviews with several dozen students (all of them Orthodox Christians unless otherwise identified) evoked comments that were similar to what we heard elsewhere with regard to a sense of personal growth and a quality education. For, example, a 14-year-old girl in seventh grade explained how her school experience changed her:

> I was very shy when I came here. I was in my world. I was what they wanted me to be to be accepted. Now, I can speak to anyone, be myself with everyone. I don't have to change to please others. I can be me.
>
> This is the best school. Teachers are more indifferent in the state schools. Here we learn. We want to learn because the teachers are more open-minded and build relationships with the students.

A 14-year-old, eighth-grade Jewish girl, born in Israel, was enrolled here because it was "highly recommended" to her parents. She "loved" the science labs and computers at the school, but also liked the "kindness" of the teachers. She mentioned how, with the segmented arrival in class of two Chinese girls, the teacher brought them over to her and they became friends.

An interview with a different Chinese girl, a 15-year-old tenth grader, revealed comparable growth in female self-worth and self-confidence. Now in her second year at this school, her parents placed her here on the recommendation of friends who had their own children enrolled.

> When I first came here, I had low self-esteem. I thought everyone was better than me. After one year though, the teachers encouraged me to show my talent, and I was able to adjust and become friendly. Now my best school friends are from India and Turkey.

Another example of the school's friendly environment came from a 12-year-old, Nigerian-Muslim eighth grader. She also found her teachers "kind and helpful" in explaining the lessons, but it was in her adjustment to school life that exemplified how empathy is as much a part of the school curriculum as the academic content:

> On the first day the teacher said to the class, 'Make her feel welcome.' That reassured me because it set the tone for the others. I'm not really

shy, but in the beginning when I don't know anyone, I am quiet. But everyone made me feel welcome, so it was easy.

A 14-year-old, eighth-grade boy also liked his teachers:

The teachers are better here. State teachers don't want to teach. Here the teachers are kind. They warn us about tests. They come to class happy.

Another contrast between the two school systems came from a 14-year-old, eighth-grade boy whose early years in a state school were "horrible."

I was picked on and humiliated. And the teachers didn't care. In fact, parents pay teachers for their children to get good grades. You don't get grades on how good you are.

A 13-year-old Romanian Muslim girl in the sixth grade offered similar comments by giving additional insights into the different school cultures:

The teachers are more friendly. They speak with us like friends. They help us. When I have a problem, they help me. Here we study better. Teachers explain more. In state schools the older kids bully the younger ones. Here the teachers protect us.

Bullying in the state schools and its virtual non-existence in Hizmet schools was a common theme we encountered. One more student comment on this subject will further serve to illustrate this point. She was a 14-year-old eight grader.

Teachers in state schools hardly ever know our names and don't help us, not with our work or with the bullying that goes on all the time. Here, if there is a fight, the teachers intervene and ask us why? Then they say or do helpful things so there is peace.

A 15-year-old, ninth-grade boy thought the teachers were "really good in anger management" and calming things down." Another 15-year-old ninth grader agreed. His parents migrated to Romania 12 years earlier during Lebanon's civil strife. Before changing to this school a year ago, he "faced a lot of bullying," but now that doesn't happen.

They teach us don't pick sides, avoid conflict, because you will only harm yourself. Words can hurt. Be careful what you say. I too was more vulgar and self-centered, but now I'm getting to be a better person.

Another 15-year-old boy was in his first year in a Romanian school. His father mostly worked abroad before returning to his native land, and so this ninth grader was previously educated in the British school system. He said the teachers make newcomers feel welcome and that he liked the smaller class sizes. The friendly help and reassurances from his teachers impressed him. In terms of his evolution as a person, his comments complemented those of the previous student:

> Because of what these teachers have instilled in me, I think a lot more now about how my words and actions have consequences.

Parents

Several parents reinforced that positive attitude about safety, such as this mother of a 14-year-old girl in the eighth grade:

> In the state school my daughter, who was shy, was a victim of bullying. They did not respect her as a person. Here, the security is very good and, not only is she getting a good education, but ethics and empathy are valued. She is happy here.

This woman learned of this school from a friend and explained that not only is her daughter happier, but she has changed from being cynical and apathetic into a highly motivated person. She made "intercultural friends easily."

Another mother of a 13-year-old eighth grader had transferred her daughter from the British school in the city because it followed "a unilateral old tradition in a one-size-fits-all" approach, was too costly, and had "a high turnover." She spoke to the "wider perspective" her daughter was developing, and praised "Educare," the regular Internet progress reports she received. She also commended the school on its security.

Financial Supporters

We met the Turkish owner of a travel agency who knew nothing about

Fethullah Gülen while growing up in Istanbul. He became acquainted with, and joined, the movement as an adult. When first asked to make a donation, he pledged $4,000 although he was only making $700 a week. His business picked up and he paid that amount in just two months, and so doubled his pledge the following year. With three children—ages 12, 15, 19—enrolled in the schools, he held a strong belief in the schools:

> There are many reasons. For one, my oldest son's behavior improved greatly in respect and motivation. I like the promotion of Turkish culture and language. I am making an investment in the future.

This man was referencing the Turkish language offered as an elective course by some schools in countries near Turkey and with close economic, social, historical, or cultural ties. Such an option makes sense in Romania, which is a neighbor via the Black Sea, has a huge common history during the Ottoman Empire, and strong trade partnerships with Turkish businesses, especially since the beginning of 1990s.

Another sponsor, one who hosted a dinner for us in his home, had no children but was one of the biggest supporters of the schools. As he passionately explained,

> I am helping Romania by helping to educate its youth. Also, my faith teaches us to be charitable, and I can't think of a better way.

Lumina: The University of South-East Europe

Opened in 2010, this university was not yet accredited when we visited it in 2014. As we learned, its educational mission paralleled other Gülen-inspired schools in using modern facilities and technology to provide a quality education in professional fields of study, while also promoting humanist values. The University was situated in a large, four-story U-shaped building, with its two wings easily as big as the main section. In addition to state-of-the-art classrooms and labs, it had seminar rooms, a conference hall, 300-seat amphitheater, library, fitness room, gymnasium, and restaurant. In addition to EU funding, the institution was supported through an umbrella organization, the Lumina Foundation (not to be confused with the same-named non-profit organization based in Indianapolis).

The university president, who previously spent five years in Bosnia spearheading the growth of another university, told us (in 2014) that they would soon have accreditation to attract international students. His goal was to increase enrollment by 50 percent as he did over a five-year period in Bosnia. So confident was the president about the appeal and potential growth of his university that he said, "Our motto is get to know us, and if you can find a better place, go there."

It appeared he subsequently achieved his goal, based on the presence of international students and expanded program offerings listed on the University's website in 2018. Sadly, this university closed soon thereafter, falling victim—like a few other Hizmet schools elsewhere—to the Erdoğan regime's pressure on friendly foreign governments to close them down, or indirectly due to the loss of financial support to sustain their operations.

While the modern, well-equipped facilities were impressive, our interests primarily lay in how this private university functioned in comparison to the public universities. From among the many graduate-level students we interviewed, five are included here to typify what we learned from the other 25 students. The comments on the next few pages thus become especially poignant because they reveal the loss of a similar educational experience in Romania to others.

Students

An older woman, married for 30 years and with a 15-year-old son, held a master's degree in business administration from the University of Bucharest, and was in a Ph.D. program here in mechanical engineering. She learned about Lumina University through the Internet, and once she began her studies found that it "exceeded my expectations." Besides praising its "very good" library and her access to "a great data base," she compared the faculty most favorably against those she had at public universities:

> The professors here are open-minded and have a wide perspective. What I like most is the human quality, their accessibility. It makes no difference who we are.

Another married woman, studying for a master's degree in business administration, also had positive comments about the faculty. Drawing from ten years of schooling in state schools, three years studying French in a private college, and three more years studying psychology in another private college, she too found the school through the Internet.

> The difference here is the friendly communication. Elsewhere students wouldn't have the courage to speak freely. With interactive methods, they stand ready to help you understand, to help you put your ideas into practice. I am very comfortable here.

A single mother in her late 30s worked as a bookkeeper and said she wanted to change her life. So, when a friend emailed her about this school, she inquired and enrolled in the business administration master's program. Her story not only echoed other compliments about teachers, but reminded us of the personal growth comments previously given by so many young people in other schools, both in Romania and elsewhere.

> If I have an idea, the teacher will listen. If I need help, it's there EVERY MOMENT *[emphasis hers]*. I am a different person now. I believe in myself. I have a vision, a direction for each way of life, personally and professionally. This came about in class and in conversations, that it is true of all of us. If you have a dream, if you can believe, it can come true. This place has been a window in my life, and I can see a teacher who can help me understand myself.

A Tatar male, in his third year and majoring in International Relations and European Studies, had an IT software career. He had previously attended a Hizmet elementary school and a state secondary school in Costanța, and offered a different contrasting slant on the two models:

> If I compare the schools, everyone gets the same message, but it is filtered through one's consciousness differently. It's all about the people who are creating the difference. You can have nice buildings and equipment, but what's behind them? The state school is like a compartmentalized factory, but in the Hizmet school, it's international and more humanistic. We talk of sharing common values, of tolerance, of helping one another. The values from Hizmet I will take with me.

Professors and Staff

We spoke to numerous professors, all of whom held a Ph.D. degree, mostly from prestigious universities in other countries, including Austria, Germany, the United Kingdom, and the United States. A few had a Hizmet elementary and/or secondary school background, but most did not. Our interactions with them did not elicit any significant difference in their teaching methodology or educational perspective. Each had his/her own disciplinary focus in the classroom, but all apparently subscribed to the prevailing academic culture of helpful, interactive learning. As far as we could tell, each felt they were in a positive work environment.

We chanced upon a web designer who had had a position with the university since 2009, and who found his work environment "family-like in helping each other." Holding degrees from Bosporus University and the University of Bucharest, he had graduated from Lumina High School when growing up in Costanța:

> My high school teachers were very friendly, and they provided an education beyond the courses. They taught us ethics and visited our homes. Even now, they call alumni and stay in touch.

Aside from the chief administrators, during our visit he was the only Hizmet school product we encountered among the university's faculty and staff. However, his comments were akin to those we heard from other alumni in other locales, thereby offering further testimony to the resilience of the seeds of tolerance, respect, and acceptance of others planted in young minds.

Retrospect

Of the four countries visited up to this point, Romania was the first in which Muslims constituted a tiny percentage of the total population. Accordingly, Hizmet school populations here contained a heavy majority of non-Muslims and few Muslims, a complete reversal of what we found in Albania, Bosnia-Herzegovina, and Kazakhstan. How would these different demographics affect the school curriculum, and the educational objectives of the Gülen-inspired schools? Of course, this was the primary research question of our field research, and Romania offered the first insight.

First, let's address the basic commonalities and differences. As in the three previous countries we visited, the native language and history were incorporated in the elementary and secondary school curricula, but the prevailing language of instruction was English. Classes in the Turkish language were also available as an optional choice. Senior administrators all were Turkish members of the Hizmet movement, and with strong educational backgrounds and experience. Now well established, the Romanian schools were primarily staffed with qualified native-born teachers and staff, not all of them directly involved in the movement.

Although teatime is an important component in Kazakh and Turkish cultures, it is not among Romanians, and so this is not a feature in the Romanian schools. Family visits by teachers—so much a part of the parent-teacher-student interaction triad mentioned in previous chapters—is rather limited in Romania due to the low number of Turkish teachers in relation to the number of students.

Also, unlike the other three countries discussed, the Hizmet international schools in Romania have a mandated religion class for one hour each week, although the content is limited to history and philosophy only. When considering the previously mentioned observations that 1) Romania is the most religious country in Europe, 2) Albania and Bosnia-Herzegovina have recent histories of religious repression and strife, and 3) Kazakhstan has a low religiosity, the inclusion here of a class in comparative religion is not that surprising. In asking students about the course content, we learned that it was non-theological and objective in presentation, and without any attempt at religious indoctrination.

In gaining permission for our interviews, we were informed that a great majority of students and parents were unlikely to recognize the name Fethullah Gülen if we were to ask questions about him. Part of it has to do with the fact that Mr. Gülen as a person is never introduced in any Hizmet-affiliated school around the world. Moreover, Mr. Gülen does not like his name to overshadow the great ideals and good work of Hizmet conducted by thousands of teachers and other volunteers. Second, bringing up such an association, given the fact that he is a cleric, might convey a religious connotation to the school's existence, the mission of which is none other than promoting ethical behavior and acceptance of others. Otherwise, such an association might cause false impression about the schools especially in countries where religion, not least Islam, has been removed from the public sphere due to historical and political reasons. In due respect to this reason, we did not mention Mr. Gülen's name in our interviews.

Parents, we learned, used the term "Turkish school" to refer to their children's school, doing so in recognition of the nationality of the administrators, the inclusion of an optional class in the Turkish language, and the school-sponsored cultural visits to Turkey. In the current climate, however, such visits are understandably not occurring at present.

What permeated all the interviews was the continuing student admiration of their teachers. Such affection might be expected from children in early childhood classes, but to find so consistent a level across all grade levels suggests that age, personality, or individual teaching style are not the relevant variables in understanding this rapport. I'll have more to say about this in the final chapter.

Romania was the first country in which dormitory students were non-existent in the schools we visited. Even though more than one-fourth of the students were bused from and to their homes, these were local schools serving the urban community. Accordingly, parental interaction with the school resembled that of U.S. schools, except on a more frequent basis. For example, instead of a one-time, back-to-school night or some other special event (e.g., parent-child dance, fundraising activity), educators involved parents more often through interactive activities (e.g., exhibits, other specially planned occasions, and online progress reports). In this way the child-parent-school triad, so much as part of Hizmet structure, was maintained even if home visits were curtailed out of necessity.

Gleaned from interviews with students, parents, educators, and financial supporters were findings that were comparable to the schools previously visited elsewhere. The Romanian schools enjoyed a strong reputation in successfully preparing students for entrance exams, further education, and professional careers. Again, and again, we heard about the teachers as role models and of their effectively developing in children a propensity to love and help others. Based on comments about students' greater open-mindedness and improved self-esteem, as well as their increased intercultural understanding and appreciation of diversity, and on to their fundraising efforts to help victims of mining disasters and earthquakes in other countries, we found that this country and its people may have been different, but the reactions matched those that we elicited in Muslim-majority countries.

References

Malathronas, John. 2014. "See Nicolae Ceausescu's Grandiose and Bloody Legacy in Bucharest." CNN. Retrieved March 1, 2021 (https://edition.cnn.com/travel/article/ceausescu-trail-bucharest-romania/index.html).

Pew Research Center. 2018. "How Do European countries differ in religious commitment?" Retrieved March 1, 2021 (https://www.pewresearch.org/fact-tank/2018/12/05/how-do-european-countries-differ-in-religious-commitment/).

"Romania." 2020. *CIA World Factbook*. Retrieved March 1, 2021 (https://www.cia.gov/library/publications/the-world-factbook/geos/ro.html).

United Nations Population Division. 2018. *World Urbanization Prospects: The 2018 Revision*. Retrieved March 1, 2021 (https://population.un.org/wup/Country-Profiles/).

6

POLAND

Poland, the fifth largest country in the European Union, has a population of almost 38 million. It shares the same unfortunate history of communist subjugation as the other four countries we visited, and like Romania, it also is a Christian country with a tiny Muslim population. However, whereas 89 percent of Romanians are Eastern Orthodox, 87 percent of the Polish people are Roman Catholics. In fact, except for the small country of Malta, Poland is the most Catholic country in Europe, with a higher proportion of Catholics than Croatia (84 percent), Italy (78 percent), Portugal (77 percent), Austria and Lithuania (75 percent), Ireland (72 percent), with France and Spain each at 60 percent (Pew Research Center 2018a).

Located in central Europe and bounded by seven nations and the Baltic Sea, Poland is about twice the size of the state of Georgia and just slightly smaller that New Mexico. Its mostly flat terrain is punctuated by the Carpathian Mountains along its southern border. Emerging from a centuries-old history of power and independence to frequent conquest and subjugation, most recently as a Soviet satellite state until 1989, Poland emerged in recent decades into a democratic country with a robust economy, the sixth largest in Europe. That economy is mostly service-based, although a large portion (about 40 percent) is industrial in such areas as manufacturing machinery, iron and steel, coal mining, chemicals, shipbuilding, food processing, glass, beverages, and textiles (*CIA World Factbook* 2020).

Societal Overview

The culture of Poland is closely connected with its intricate thousand-year history. Its unique character developed as a result of its geography at the confluence of various European regions. With origins in the culture of the Early Slavs, over a period of time it has been profoundly influenced by cultures within the Germanic, Latinate and Byzantine worlds, and to some degree by the many other ethnic groups and minorities living in Poland.

Catholicism plays an important role in the lives of many Polish citizens, with 61 percent reporting that they attend mass at least once monthly, which is the highest among all European countries. In terms of religiosity, 40 percent describe themselves as "highly religious," compared to 55 percent in Romania. That religiosity extends to controversial social issues, such as abortion and gay marriage, which are opposed by at least half of all Poles (Pew Research Center 2018b).

Other religion groups in Poland include Muslims and about 10,000 Jews. There has been a continuous presence of Islam in Poland since the 14th century with the influx of Tatars, a Turkic-speaking people, most of whom still reside in west-central Russia. Apart from these traditional Tatar communities, Poland has also become home since the 1970s to a small but growing immigrant and native-born Muslim community, particularly after the overthrow of Communism in 1989 and the end of government's repression of religion. Since then, Muslim immigrants from Turkey and the former Yugoslavia have come to Poland. Currently, the total number of Muslims in Poland is estimated at approximately 41,400 Sunni Muslims (Bieńkowska 2019). Sadly, in recent years anti-Muslim sentiment had been on the rise (Pędziwiatr 2018). Like citizens in other Eastern European countries, Poles are less likely than those in Western Europe willing to accept Muslims as part of their family—33 percent in Poland willing compared one-half to three-fourths in Western European countries (Pew Research Center 2018c). Such findings suggest that limited cross-cultural social acceptance or interaction, making the interview results in Hizmet schools in Poland of particular interest.

Schools and Administrators

Before visiting Hizmet schools in Warsaw, we spent an afternoon with Eugeniusz Sakowicz, a Polish Catholic theologian and Professor of Theological Sciences and Chair of the Department of Religiology and Ecumenism at the Institute of Dialogue of Culture and Religion at the Faculty of Theology of Cardinal S. Wyszyński University in Warsaw. That extensive title is well suited for this religious scholar who has authored a dozen books and more than 400 scientific publications, including several on Islam and on the Gülen movement (2002, 2007, 2018). We spoke to him at great length about his writings on Hizmet.

> I want to demystify fears about Islam, to change the reader's mind, and not be terrorized by the news. I want people to find common values. It's hard to discuss things with people who hate us. By looking at Islam, I learn more about my own culture. You can't change all minds, just take a small step and hope it makes a difference.

On what intrigued him about the Hizmet movement, he made several points directly relevant to our field research, such as:

> I like the idea of Gülen's interfaith dialogue. He puts his trust in children. Our generation will not change the world, but they can.

How, then, did he think the Hizmet schools play a role in preparing a new generation?

> These schools are distinctive with their high level of science. They have the best students and see that they are well educated in these fields. And, importantly, it is a good place for different cultures to be together without conflict.

He also stressed that it was the educators, even more than the curriculum, who were the critical element:

> Most important are the teachers, even how they live their private lives. And, these teachers have experience in several countries; they are more cosmopolitan. That is important for students in this global market.

That highly informative and productive exchange served as a helpful prelude for a visit the next day to Meridian High School. It is one of four components of schools operating under the Meridian Foundation, an umbrella organization that is comparable in structure and functioning to those in other countries. There is also a kindergarten and elementary school nearer the city center, unlike this middle school and high school on the city outskirts. The high school vice principal was Turkish and part of the movement, like almost all administrators. Asked about the dual mission of the school (providing a quality education along with the promotion of ethical values and tolerance), he explained:

> A person with a positive idea about different others cannot act against them. We try to familiarize students with the idea to see and respect persons from different cultures.

Since its establishment in 2002, this school has been drawing the attention of parents and educators because of the outstanding academic performance of its students. It also hosts the Meridian Mathematic Contest, where high school students from throughout Poland come to compete. Another factor in the school's prestige is its international student body. As one might expect, more than half of the students were Polish, who had classmates who were Turkish, Vietnamese, Canadian and Mongolian, comprising another 40 percent of the remaining student population. Parents came from many walks of life, but included numerous non-Polish parents who were in the diplomatic corps or corporate executives, while some native-born parents were civic leaders. Of the 28 teachers, 11 are full-time and four are Turkish. Four others are foreign nationals (England, Ireland, Mongolia, and Turkmenistan).

On a subsequent visit to the elementary school, the principal explained that 14 is the average class size, although a few higher grades may have 20. The typical acceptance rate is 30 out of 45 applicants for each grade. Almost three-fourths of the students are Polish, but also enrolled were non-Polish students from 25 other countries, whose parents work in Poland. Among the 30 teachers, only three were Turkish and most others Polish. Like public schools, the school follows a national curriculum structure, but with classes both in Polish and English. School personnel maintain a "very close relationship" with parents. Extra school activities are similar to those in the United States, but one special event was the regularly scheduled "Saturday Harmony Breakfast," which is held separately for each class level.

Teachers

A Polish fourth-grade teacher, holder of a master's degree from a public university, had 14 years teaching experience, ten of those years here. She felt that she was more than a teacher, and so she dealt with "both the mind and the heart." All cultures are different, she said, and she wanted to create a bridge for her students: to listen, organize activities, get them to respond.

> All students are personal to me. They need rules, but you strike a balance and let them feel free to ask questions, give opinions. If I promise I will help, I do. I may stay here all day and into the night sometimes. And I know all my parents by name. I may call or email them, and each day I send them the daily attendance register, so they know their children are here and safe.

A second-grade teacher, with B.A. and M.A. degrees from public universities and 25 years of experience in a public school, answered a job-opening advertisement when the school opened nine years earlier. With her two children now grown, she welcomed the opportunity to live and work in Warsaw. Clearly, her background enabled her to make comparisons:

> The biggest difference is that everything here is new, so available, and easy to find. It's harder for a teacher to make students curious without the right material.... These children come from more affluent families and the parents take more interest.... All of us are really involved in those key words you see on the lobby signs [e.g., tolerance, equality] .... It's hard for a child from a different country to feel accepted, to advance to the next level with no mixing. Here we utilize cooperative, interactive methods so race, religion, nationality are not barriers to empathy.

A non-practicing English Anglican—married to a Polish Catholic and with a one-year-old son—came here two years ago to teach English and math in grades three to six. After several years of teaching experience in South Africa and at a British International School in Europe, he visited a friend in Warsaw and liked the city so much, he decided to stay. What he liked most about this school was "the closeness of the staff and kids." He found everyone friendlier and the school functioning for "the total person."

The teacher/pedagogue and school psychologist work together for the child. I am more than a teacher. I am a confidante, a friend, someone dealing with education, but also social skills and interaction. For example, we had a kid who stole some pencils from another kid and was publicly caught. We brought the whole class into the discussion, did some role playing, talked about respect, patience, tolerance. We had that kid become part of the crafts club and help others, including distributing colored pencils. It all worked out beautifully.

An Uzbek teacher, married to a woman from Turkmenistan and the mother of his two daughters, has taught in the middle school for four years. Introduced to the Hizmet movement in the ninth grade, he previously taught for six years in Turkmenistan, which was quite different.

In Turkmenistan, there is a closer bond between parents and teachers. The mindset is "my child is your child." Here people keep their distance, keep their trust within their own circle.

Asked what keeps him in the Hizmet movement here in Poland, he replied.

It's trying to give the world peace and harmony. It might seem very slow or unimportant, but I see a lot of places where this fellowship is being achieved. And one day in the future it will indeed lead to world peace. As an individual, I am trying to do whatever I can with my strength to contribute.

A Polish Catholic woman with a public-school education up through her master's degree, had seven years teaching experience at this school. Her enthusiasm for teaching was evident: "It keeps you young. I love talking to young people." She liked the smaller class sizes and international element of the school, but found the parents less involved than those during her six years of public-school teaching before coming here, perhaps prompting some of these comments:

I am more than a teacher. I have to be a counselor and psychiatrist too. We teach tolerance and values, but interweave them with the educational program.

All teachers spoke to the higher socioeconomic status of families sending their children here, but differed in their perceptions of student motivation and parental involvement.

Students

A 15-year-old ninth grader, who was raised as a Muslim, had a Turkish father who was a textile storeowner and a Polish mother who was a housewife. Her father knew the school principal and she had been enrolled since the first grade. Commuting daily by car driven by her grandmother, she had hopes of a college education abroad. Her favorite subject was geography and she enjoyed the extra-curricular activities of volleyball and tennis. She was the first of many students here to describe her teachers positively for their tolerance and helpfulness.

That view was comparable to one that was expressed by another ninth grader, a Polish Catholic. Her father owned a plastics company and mother was a housewife, but she was the one who decided to come to this school after graduating from a public elementary school. She heard about the school from a friend and was "excited" about the chance to meet different people.

> There are international students here. It's great! We quickly learn it's not how people look, but their personalities. Also, teachers—French, Italian, German, Chinese. They are friendly, accept differences. We can talk with them. In hard times, they care about us. We trust each other, teacher and student. It's a really good place to study.

With her sights set on an acting career and a college education abroad, one could easily imagine this outgoing young woman—commuting via a one-way, 25-minute subway ride, and taking six-hour singing and dancing lessons on Saturdays and Sundays—as someone who may well realize her dream. Certainly, she revealed herself to be a happy and dedicated person in her interview.

Another Polish Catholic student who was the one to pick this school, not his parents, was a 14-year-old ninth grader. First attending a Canadian middle school in Warsaw, he left because the teachers "had no passion for giving information." He saw the level of his education declining there and "needed to learn more."

The teachers here teach you so you can understand. What's important is that they teach you the basics, including compassion, empathy, caring, asking questions. When I first came here, everyone tried to show off. Now, everyone is nicer, more accepting of others. For example, I see the 5-6 Jewish students here treated nicely by the Muslim students. We are like a big family.

A 16-year-old Polish Catholic ninth grader was born in Krakow. However, she lived in Prague for six years and attended the British school there. Now enrolled in this school, she was unhappy it did not offer art classes, necessitating her taking private classes. She also thought that her teachers in Czechia trusted students more, not mentioning cheating so much, something she "never thought of." Still, she liked the openness of the school environment:

> This school is more tolerant of other cultures. There is better respect. The teachers don't really talk about it. It's not taught. The reality of differences is there, but the way everyone mixes is very positive.

Parents

One Polish-Catholic father of two middle school boys, fourth and sixth graders, held a degree in economics from Poznań University and worked as a corporate fund manager, as well as financial advisor to the school. He found the school through the Internet and became enamored with its small class sizes, quality, and educational climate. Not only did the schools "push very hard" for students to study, but even did that through sports and academic competitions. Also, twice a year the parents and teachers will play sports together.

> I like the close relationship the school has with us parents. I feel like a member there, not like a client. It really is an international school where the students and parents can meet others. This school instills self-discipline and motivation. My sons are willing to stay longer for extra help, like preparing for entrance exams.

A Polish-Catholic mother, the graduate of a public university and holding a middle management position in an electric company, had two sons ages 6 and 11 enrolled. Although the school had the full Polish school curriculum enabling her to transfer them to the public school if there was a problem, she said would never do so because of the "well-liked and really good teachers" who are "fair and well-prepared." What she liked most, though, was that "different cultures mix here, even some exotic ones I never heard of before."

> Skin color and religions don't matter. That would never happen in other schools. They have a monthly evaluative contest with the theme of tolerance. In May, they hold International Day, where each class takes a country. There are decorations, songs, poems, and so on. Students visit each other with their parents. I really like it.

Another Polish-Catholic father whose wife is a computer programmer, was the graduate of a private university in Warsaw and now a corporate manager. Through Internet research, his wife had identified this school as best for their daughter, then in the third grade. Although a bit unhappy by the frequent changing of teachers from one year to the next (something mentioned by two other parents), he liked their rapport with the children, approachability, and rapid response to any inquiries. Like other parents, he praised the emphasis on English lessons, the extra attention because of smaller class sizes, and the international student composition that "open minds to other cultures."

> My daughter had an African-American teacher and described her to us not by her skin color, but by her hair style. Also, my daughter experienced a little bullying but the teacher nipped it in the bud when we complained. And, another thing, there are so many extra-curricular activities here, and more for kids waiting for their parents to pick them up after classes are over.

We also met a Turkish father of three children: a son in the fourth grade, another in high school, and a daughter in a university. A college graduate, married to a woman he met in Croatia, his company transferred him to Poland two years earlier. Not active in the movement but influenced by it, he described his transformation:

> When I was younger, I was self-centered with a one-sided view of the world. I thought I knew it all. I had a friend in the Gülen movement and, through him, I listened to some of the talks. In time, my values changed. I

went from just a personal standpoint to seeing different angles. The world became richer, more colorful. I want my children to have these values. These schools are a special comfort to me, because my children's needs are met and the educators' lifestyle has meaning and impact.

He also discussed about how he liked the teaching of the importance of hard work but also ethics. Although not a school sponsor in the usual sense, he had given a scholarship in addition to his donations to the Red Cross.

Financial Supporters

We had private breakfast meetings with different Turkish businessmen in Poland who were financial supporters of Hizmet schools in their adopted country. These were decidedly pleasant encounters, both in terms of the food spread laid before us, and the friendly conversations. All were members of the Federation of Turkish Businessmen in Poland, which we were told met occasionally but not very often.

The first of these breakfast meetings was with three co-owners of a large meat packaging company. One of them was a 27-year-old former professional soccer player, whose father had sent him to a Hizmet school as a young man. One of the other partners, about 20 years older, said, "I knew I could trust him as a partner because, with his Hizmet education, I knew he would never cheat me."

A 35-year-old owner of a towel-manufacturing factory migrated here from Montenegro but grew up in Turkey. In explaining his involvement in the movement and his financial backing of these schools in Poland, he offered an interesting observation:

> Hizmet picks up the mountains between us and builds the bridge. As human beings, we all have the same goals. For Hizmet, there is no nation, no races, only humans united together. For me, there was a big distance between Christians and Muslims before I met Hizmet. Now I can connect easily. Hizmet gives us meaning and values.

Another morning we chatted with two partners in the underwear manufacturing. They too spoke of their satisfaction in helping to fund the schools, as one of them said, "I want Hizmet to be the voice of Islam, not of those who promote violence."

On a separate occasion we met a Turkish engineer who worked in Russia before settling in Poland. Married and with a six-year-old daughter, he was not a sponsor but his company contributed to a few school events during the year. As a young man he had attended public schools, with 60 students in a class sitting four abreast. His teachers "taught only rules and fear," and he became a "troublemaker," he told us, and so his parents sent him to a Hizmet school.

> They taught me I could make something out of nothing. There was no ideology—ever. They just taught us how to live a life, with inspired discipline—motivation—strong values. They made me a better person.

Although influenced by it, he is not active in the Hizmet movement "because it takes time that I don't have," but declared that he likes it and its network of mutual helping.

A 40-year-old Turkish businessman, owner of a management consulting firm with clients worldwide, also was not in the movement although he went to Hizmet schools. Because he "likes the teaching of moderate Islam and modernity," his company gave financial support to several school events annually. He said his conservative detractors in Turkey didn't like his helping Christians and Jews, but "they are the ones who are wrong." He also shared this interesting anecdote:

> In my business I travel extensively. Recently I was in Saudi Arabia to meet with a Somali, the key man in his company, to broker their purchase of a $100,000 German product. After some pleasant conversation about ourselves to establish a relationship. I prepared to make my presentation. He stopped me, saying that he didn't need to see and hear it, that he was happy to do business with a Turk with Hizmet schooling. Why? He also was a graduate from a Hizmet school, and said, "I know you would never lie or sell me a bad product." That's how we are with one another. Wouldn't this be a wonderful world, if everyone was like that?

Vistula University

Begun in 1992, Vistula University moved to its modern campus in 2009 and, at the time of our visit, had an enrollment of 4,500 students, with

70 percent undergraduates and 30 percent at the graduate level. In conversations with the university president and other administration officials, we learned that, after communism, little was happening in higher education, but about 200 small colleges opened. Lacking high standards and fundraising capabilities, most soon disappeared. In contrast, Vistula University (now one of the oldest non-public universities in Poland and fully accredited) began operations with business partners with banking, communications, and energy groups, many of them Turkish. In contrast to Muslim-majority countries where all donations are anonymous, here they were publicized on the University's website. Originally intended to be temporary financial supporters until the debt was paid off, when the University became self-sufficient in 2015, about two dozen companies remain as financially supportive partners.

Hizmet values were evident in the comments of various administrators:

> Our mission on universal values is through a low-key approach. For example, we had a problem recently with cheating/plagiarism. Some students were writing essays copied from *Wikipedia*. We had to teach them about academic honesty, by making an analogy to stealing and reminding them that taking what is not theirs makes them less a person and cheats them out of becoming more creative and accomplished because they didn't give themselves the opportunity to learn and grow.

Related comments came from others. One Dean opined, "We invest in a new generation, be the engine for economic growth, but not at the expense of moral values." Another official said:

> When you have good intentions by planting knowledge in a new group and just leave it, that's not enough. Trouble may follow. We try to create upright individuals and keep them that way after they leave us.

In our speaking to another university administrator about her involvement, she noted, "Gülen has a plan for good people to advance civilization through modern education. I was intrigued by that plan and wanted to be part of it."

In line with her remarks, but not aware of them, the university president perhaps best summed up the commitment these educators have made in their careers when he said, "We could make more money in the business world, but we are part of a vision for the betterment of humanity."

Professors

An Uzbek teacher, with a Ph.D. in economics from a public university, was in his second year of teaching at Vistula. He gave some insight into his life as a student in a Hizmet school. As a boy in his native land, he was one of about a thousand applicants taking the entrance exam in 1998. He placed 22nd among the 60 who were accepted into an all-boys school. Then twelve, he lived in a dormitory from Sunday evening until Friday at 1 p.m. Homesick, he cried for a month, but his father told him that if he wanted goals, he had to do this. Older boys encouraged him not to give up, and in time he adjusted and had "a good experience there, both socially and educationally." Years later at Vistula, while studying for his master's degree, other Uzbeks introduced him to the Hizmet movement. That is a rather interesting fact, because living as an impressionable youth in a near-total institution as a resident student, he was not recruited (critics might claim "indoctrinated") into the movement. Rather, he spoke of "exposure to an ethical way of life" and only as an adult did he come to know about the Hizmet movement, which he now fully supported.

> These are good people, accepting one another like brothers. I wish all people could see the world like this. Christians, Muslims, and Jews should sit together and discuss their commonalities. We cannot solve our problems otherwise.

A Polish instructor with degrees in accounting liked the open-door policy up through the chancellor that allowed for the exchange of ideas. She spoke to their "management by objective" as they "strive with flexibility to meet the goals of a "quality education, one that builds self-confidence, and develops understanding."

> I like this place. Poland has many problems with its educational system, so we try to be the best, not just in transmitting knowledge, but also respect for others. For example, the Ukrainian students here have difficulty making friends, just like my Slovakian students. Through group projects they see that they are similar.

Students

Most students were Polish, but about 15 other nationalities were also en-rolled, particularly from Russia and Ukraine. Only two small dormito-ries with a total of 50 beds then existed, with other students housed in nearby hostels. Most students were commuters and we witnessed many in their arriving and leaving by public transportation means.

An Australian freshman gave voice to the rapport between stu-dents and faculty. She was the only child of a Lebanese father and Polish mother (both Christians), and had a public-school education back home. She came to Poland on holiday and stayed with her grandparents while checking out the university. Through an Internet search, it was the only school she found with a School of Tourism and Hospitality Management. It took three months for her to get cleared for admission and she found her adjustment to a new culture "very hard." However, with classes in English, the presence of other international students, and a program she wanted, life became easier. Another big factor was the faculty:

> They are always here to help you, answer your questions. They are helpful and reliable, always there for you, even if they're busy, espe-cially the Turkish professors.

A Ukrainian Catholic sophomore, majoring in international rela-tions, chose Vistula University after an Internet search and reading about the school, its faculty and ranking. He too found his first weeks "terribly difficult," because he felt "different as a Ukrainian," but knew he "would survive." His teachers helped him feel more accepted.

> I like them. They are so professional. There's no politics. They always help us to find our way if we have problems. They tell us, "Be brave. You are not alone.

Another sophomore majoring in international relations had at-tended Hizmet schools in his native Kazakhstan. Although offered a college scholarship there, he opted instead "for a new culture" and "this school has a really good reputation." He found his professors similar in many ways to his former teachers, although he liked better here the blend of the practical ("many projects") with the theoretical. Planning to earn a master's degree in economics in yet another country (Canada,

Germany, or the United States), he felt good about the education he was getting, but also revealed a bit about how the second Hizmet goal about values affected him.

> We learn "never give up," that all is achievable. Here I developed even more tolerance than before. I learned Western experiences—French, Spanish, Polish, Ukrainian cultures. Now I know, more than ever, that the future lies in the people.

Not knowing English or Polish when he first arrived, and with no experience with the Hizmet movement, a Turkish-Muslim junior told of his "terrible" first weeks. A product of Turkish public schools, including two years in vocational school, he came to Vistula University after an Internet search revealed it as the "most popular private university of high quality." Working his way through college in IT, his goal was to create a software company in Turkey after he graduated. Echoing other students about the differences between past and current teachers, he revealed his experiences with them:

> My old teachers never encouraged anything. They just taught stuff and either you got it or you didn't. Here I am getting a high-quality education, and my teachers, the Turkish ones especially, stay late to help us. Not only do they give us examples from their lectures, but they've helped me get past the Arabic terrorist stereotype, something I have great difficulty getting my father (a retired soldier) to understand.

A sophomore Ukrainian Catholic spent her sophomore high school year as an exchange student in England and that experience, together with the similarities in the Ukrainian and Polish languages, eased her adjustment to studying in Warsaw. Moreover, with long-range plans to earn a master's degree in Canada and then work for an international corporation, she wanted a college education in a multicultural setting. Her new experience in a Hizmet school environment (she didn't use that terminology) offered a strong contrast to what she previously knew:

> Teachers in public schools had prejudices. Here we have different religions. It's totally different. Every person is unique. I get new knowledge and different points of view. I think one way, then hear another. The teachers encourage this.

A Polish graduate student with a public-school background through his undergraduate years liked the opportunities that Vistula provided for personal development:

> In the public schools I was not forced to do anything I didn't like. My comfort zone wasn't taken away from me. Here I am forced to speak/work with others, which helped me become more self-confident. My teachers pay more attention, not just in the subject matter, but in developing yourself, improving your communication skills…. I also like being surrounded by foreigners—Turks, Ukrainians, and Russians.

Another Polish graduate student also majoring in international relations was a single male in his mid-twenties. Commenting along similar lines about the intercultural contacts, he reflected on his metamorphosis:

> This contact with foreigners changed me completely. I don't like my old friends anymore because they didn't change at all. For example, my opinion of Turks and Muslims is different. It's not just kebabs and radicals. I know many now and my perspective has changed.

A Polish first-year graduate economics major had no knowledge or connection to the Hizmet movement, but nonetheless subconsciously identified with its concepts:

> Meeting challenges of political polarization, economic inequalities, and racism requires critical thinking and openness in educational institutions. I find that here.

It was unclear what influenced her thinking about societal problems, but her comments attested to her finding a learning environment compatible with them.

Retrospect

As was the case in Romania, Muslims represent a minute portion of the total population in Poland. Consequently, the Hizmet schools here, particularly at the elementary and secondary school levels, were heavily enrolled with non-Muslim students. However, Poland's economy is twice stronger than that of Romania in terms of average income and Gross

Domestic Product (*World Population Review* 2020). Therefore, although these two countries were similar as Christian countries (though of different dominant faiths), they were dissimilar in terms of population affluence. Certainly, both were different from the three Muslim-dominant countries covered in previous chapters. How the school curriculum and Hizmet educational objectives fared in Poland and compared with Romania comprised another phase of our cross-cultural research.

What was reported for Romania held equally true for Poland. A mostly Polish faculty and staff worked under administrations headed by Turkish-born educators. Courses in the Turkish language were optional choices, and courses on Polish history and culture were offered in the native language, while all other courses were conducted in English. Family visits were rare but replaced by an ongoing interaction with parents through regular progress reports, phone and online interactions, and special events to draw parent to the schools, such as Turkish dinner nights and invitational activities akin to back-to-school nights in the United States. Similarly, such activities are more frequent at the elementary school level.

As in Romania, a weekly one-hour class in religion is taught by part-time teachers, women authorized by the Catholic Church to do so. However, parents may choose to have their children take an ethics class instead, and that is taught by a full-time teacher employed by the school. This arrangement offers more flexibility for families in Poland.

Like their Romanian counterparts, these parents referred to the Hizmet schools as "Turkish schools." Almost all were from a higher socioeconomic background than many Romanians we interviewed, not surprisingly, given the economic differences between the two countries. They believed the tuition costs paid for their children's education was well worth the price in return for the school providing a quality education in a safe environment. Like their children, they admired the dedication, friendliness, and competence of the teaching staff.

At the university level, we found students and faculty who had been introduced to the Hizmet movement in their youth but, by and large, most were not involved. Many faculty members were hired through the normal search process, telling us they were attracted by the modern facilities and satisfying work environment. Students chose to attend, they typically said, because of the university's reputation, its modern facilities and programs available, and/or the convenience of location. With virtually no college dormitories, the students—like those in the lower grades—commuted by private or public transportation to get their education. International students—either attending through Erasmus (a European Union student exchange program) or recruited by university representatives in their home country—found housing accommodations through the University. Although many spoke favorably of their classes and professors, none spoke of any political or religious persuasive efforts by anyone connected with the school.

Polish culture and lifestyle did play a part in how the Hizmet schools functioned but not, as far as we could tell, in their primary mission or goals. Those twin objectives of providing a quality education and promoting empathy for others who are different were effectively achieved, as repeatedly shown in our conversations with students, educators, parents, and financial supporters. However, as reported in this chapter, some teachers with life experiences in several cultures did note that the parent-teacher bond was not as close as in other Hizmet schools.

References

Bieńkowska Anna, et al. 2019. "Religious Denominations in Poland 2015-2018." Retrieved December 15, 2021 (https://ec.europa.eu/eurostat/web/main/data).

Narkowicz, Kasia and Konrad Pędziwiatr. 2017. "Why Are Polish People So Wrong About Muslims in Their Country?" *Open Democracy*. Retrieved March 1, 2021 (https://www.opendemocracy.net/en/can-europe-make-it/why-are-polish-people-so-wrong-about-muslims-in/).

Pędziwiatr, Konrad. 2018. "The Catholic Church in Poland on Muslims and Islam." *Patterns of Prejudice* 52:5 (461-478).

Pew Research Center, 2018a. "5 Facts About Catholics in Europe." Retrieved March 1, 2021 (https://www.pewresearch.org/fact-tank/2018/12/19/5-facts-about-catholics-in-europe/).

Pew Research Center. 2018b. "How do European countries differ in religious commitment?" Retrieved March 1, 2021 (https://www.pewresearch.org/fact-tank/2018/12/05/how-do-european-countries-differ-in-religious-commitment/).

Pew Research Center. 2019c. "Eastern and Western Europeans Differ on Importance of Religion, Views of Minorities, and Key Social Issues." Retrieved March 1, 2021 (https://www.pewforum.org/2018/10/29/eastern-and-western-europeans-differ-on-importance-of-religion-views-of-minorities-and-key-social-issues).

"Poland." 2020. *CIA World Factbook*. Retrieved March 1, 2021 (https://www.cia.gov/library/publications/the-world-factbook/geos/pl.html).

Sakowicz, Eugeniusz. 2002. *Is Islam a Terrorist Religion?* Krakow, Poland: Homo Dei Publishing House.

Sakowicz, Eugeniusz. 2007. *Talks on Islam and Dialogue*. Lublin, Poland: Polyhymnia Publishing House

Sakowicz, Eugeniusz. 2018. "The Resolution of Conflicts and Building Unity: M. Fethullah Gülen's Pedagogical Proposition." Pp. 3-28. In *The Hizmet Movement and Peacebuilding: Global Cases*. Edited by Mohammed Abu-Nimer and Timothy Seidel. Lanham, MD: Rowman & Littlefield.

World Population Review. 2020a. "GDP Ranked by Country 2020." Retrieved March 1, 2021 (https:// worldpopulationreview.com/countries/).

World Population Review. 2020b. "Median Income by Country 2020." Retrieved March 1, 2021 https://worldpopulationreview.com/country-rankings/median-income-by-country).

7

CANADA AND THE UNITED STATES

To complete our cross-cultural field research, we selected two obvious choices known for their secular macrocultures and their multicultural population compositions. The Canadian and U.S. governments have always promoted freedom of religion, and both countries long have been destination choices for millions of migratory peoples from all parts of the world. At the time of this research, Canada was receiving about 350,000 immigrants each year, and about one million newcomers were entering the United States. Our expectation was that the Hizmet schools would more likely contain mostly children of immigrants rather than native-born parents. How would that affect the curriculum and mission of the schools?

Canada

Bordering two oceans and the northern neighbor to the United States, Canada is a land of vast distances, but it contains continuous permafrost that makes development rather difficult. Thus, almost all 35+ million Canadians live within 190 miles of the southern border with the United States. The Canadian provinces with the greatest population concentrations are Ontario (13 million), Quebec (8 million), and British Columbia at 4.6 million (Sawe 2019).

Canada has two official languages, English and French, and many Canadians are bilingual. About 22 percent of Canadians speak French as their primary language, most especially in Quebec Province. Throughout the rest of the country, about 58 percent use English as their first language. The remaining languages are scattered among recent immigrants from Asian, Europe, and the Middle East, as well as the indigenous peoples, who constitute about four percent.

Although this country's form of government differs from that of the United States, its economy is fairly similar. Canada is part of the English Commonwealth, with a Governor General serving as agent for Queen Elizabeth II. He appoints each of the 105 senators, who each serve lifetime appointments until age 75. The House of Commons members are elected directly by their district constituencies for four-year terms. A land of abundant natural resources (third in the world in oil reserves and the seventh-largest oil producer), Canada has a highly skilled labor force and a market-based economic system. It is the largest foreign supplier of energy (natural gas, oil, electric power) to the United States, which also imports about three-fourths of Canada's merchandise (CIA World Factbook 2020).

Societal Overview

Data from the 2016 Census revealed about one-third of the population identified themselves as non-ethnic Canadians. Among those self-identifying with single or multiple ancestry were 18 percent English, 14 percent Scottish, French and Irish at 13+ percent, German 10 percent, Italian five percent, and First Nations four percent (Sawe 2019). Religious groupings were: Catholic 39 percent, Protestant 29 percent, and 24 percent atheist or agnostic. Most prevalent among the minority religions was Islam at three percent and Hinduism at two percent (Oberheu 2018). About 20,000 of the 50,000 Turkish Canadians live in Greater Toronto.

Despite religious affiliation, a 2018 survey found that 64 percent of Canadian adults thought that religion had a less important role in their country than it did 20 years ago. One-in-five reported attending a weekly religious service, while 24 percent seldom did, and 25 percent said they never did, and 36 percent said they never pray. Even so, more than half (55 percent) said religion remained at least somewhat important in their lives, including about three-in-ten (29 percent) who said it is very important to them. The latter is higher than those in the UK, France and most other Western European countries. By all of these measures, young Canadian adults are less religious than their elders (Pew Research Center 2019a).

Nile Academy

At the time of our visit in 2015, Nile Academy had three campuses; a boys' school (Plunkett Campus), a girls' school (Scarborough Campus), and a girls' high school with co-ed K-8 grades (Blue Haven Campus). One year later, the Plunkett and Scarborough Campuses were shut down, and merged into Blue Haven to form a single school on a single campus. In 2015, though, over a two-day period we visited all three schools, and at that time, no minimum score, not even an entrance exam was required for students to attend.

The girls' school, offering grades 1 through 12, began in 2005 had an enrollment of 300, with 23 nationalities represented, Somalis heavily so in the elementary grades. Among high school students, 33 nationalities were enrolled, especially from Turkey, Iraq, and Syria. Only 15-20 students attended on scholarships. Most of the students were Muslims. Half of the 27 mostly non-Muslim teachers were born in Canada, and seven were Turkish.

Although sex education classes are offered in Canadian public high schools, that is not the case at Nile Academy, which is a private school and receives no government funding. However, the high school must meet Canadian standards, requiring 18 credits, 15 of which are in mandated fields, including four credits English, three in math, two in science, and one each in Canadian history, Canadian geography, the arts, health and physical education. The remaining three credits are in a variety of choices in several fields, such as the arts, business, cooperative education, science, social science, and technology education.

The school's Azerbaijani-born principal went to York University and had an M.A. degree in linguistic, then taught English in a Hizmet school for several years. He told us that the school had no comparative religion class but offered one in "social ethics." This class is really one in Islamic values," he explained and added, "The parents requested this course, because they feared the loss of traditions. They want the kids to be integrated but not assimilated."

The principal of the boys' high school came straight from Turkey in 2005 to become its only head administrator thus far. The school had only 85 students but had set a goal of reaching 700 (a goal partly achieved by the aforementioned merger of three schools). All but two of the students

were Muslims, and half the teachers were Turkish Canadians who had lived in Canada for a good number of years. He mentioned some of the students would be participating in an Olympiad Science Fair in Texas that coming weekend.

Teachers

A math teacher/guidance counselor, was a graduate of public schools and earned his B.S. degree in chemical engineering, but chose a teaching career. He came to Toronto after his brother's friend invited him, and he was clearly fervent about what he was doing.

> It is more than teaching, more than a mission. Look at what is happening in the world with the stereotyped view of Muslims. I don't want kids to be ashamed to be a Muslim. Each can be a part of this country and be Muslims too. We are all brothers and sisters. If you live what you believe, we can bring peace. How we teachers behave is important. Kids are great observers. When they see what you are doing, caring for them and patient, they have good role models. Some people do things for money. The people here feel. They are there for you.

A female math teacher, who emigrated from Turkey in 2005, talked about weekly staff meetings where all can become aware of any student problems to prevent anyone "isolated from issues affecting them." A Catholic science teacher, born and educated in the United States, told how they help students overcome academic or personal problems to ensure their success. A third teacher discussed the school's *in loco parentis* responsibility and teachers' compassion for foreign students to learn English to overcome their social isolation. "We do everything," he said, including sports, barbeques, watching movies that the kids suggest, and sharing teatime stories."

A male math teacher from Turkey, who taught in Kazakhstan previously for seven years, found the students in Canada less motivated and less socially outgoing. He thought the school's limited facilities affected the monotony some felt. [Note: the merging of the three schools since then appears to have overcome this factor.] He too spoke about *in loco parentis* as an important element in being a Hizmet educator:

Sending your child overseas to study is a big risk. It's hard for parents and difficult at first for the student. If it's bad here, they won't come back. Intercultural friendships are not easy at first, but over time we can gather all aspect together. For example, there is teatime when we can be informal and talk about all kinds of things. And, after fasting during Ramadan, a shared dinner with others helps bring us closer together.

A social science teacher, with degrees from York University and Western Reserve University, began his teaching career at Nile Academy two years earlier. A Christian and fifth-generation Canadian, he was married and had two young children. In comparing his own educational experience with his current situation, he told us that the teachers here were "more personally engaged," and gave examples of hugging, driving students to places, and taking them on camping trips. Asked about student intercultural relationships, he ventured the thought that Turkish-Canadian and Turkish students do get along, but the former seemed to favor the Somali students more than do the Turkish students.

A chemistry teacher/guidance counselor, graduate of a public university in Turkey and mother of two young children (ages 5 and 7), provided additional insights into the school from a staff perspective:

> For our Turkish students we provide culture and language maintenance, and we offer them food choices in the cafeteria not available in the public schools. We have university students who tutor on Saturdays as unpaid volunteers. The teachers are also dedicated, always volunteering for after-school activities.

Her remarks were further amplified by the school psychologist, a woman who arrived from Turkey in 2010. She and her husband, who was the director of the Intercultural Dialogue Institute, also had two young children (ages 2 and 6).

> We provide a culturally safe environment in this multicultural society. There is less confusion because the students can know their teachers. The cultural barrier doesn't stop me from celebrating Canadian history with them, or holding events to celebrate Christmas, Halloween, or giving candies during Eid [end of Ramadan fasting]. Our students are not isolated. They watch TV, go places. We explain to the kids what is

right and wrong. We can shape our own culture and make something even better. We give good character education. Love, patience, and tolerance are the key foundations of Hizmet.

We spoke to two of those student volunteers. The first was in his third year at York University where he was double majoring in political science and public administration. A Kurd who left Turkey in 2010, he actually tutored on Monday-Wednesday-Friday afternoons when he didn't have classes. He also spoke of his participation in the twice-weekly mandated teatime sessions, organizing soccer games, table tennis competitions, and taking students on picnics.

A young woman, who graduated from Nile Academy after beginning in the seventh grade, now held a B.A. degree in psychology from York University. Both her parents were from Turkey, and she was now a tutor to the students with long-range plans of becoming a teacher herself. One Turkish tradition she included with her students was teatime sessions. In speaking about her past experience as a student and now part of the staff, she spoke about students treated like family, with contact continuing even after they graduate through reunions and email. Offering comments similar to those of students in other countries, she said:

> This place was my first education where teachers cared about you. There is no bullying here, something my friends experience in public schools. Also, I was more assertive, less friendly before I came here. Students are both beloved and taught to respect others. Class sizes are smaller and you learn more. You must pay to go here, but you definitely get your money's worth.

Asked how she thought the school might have changed her, this young woman wasn't able to say much about that. As the interviews continued the next day though, she approached and handed me a note, explaining she had time to reflect on this question and wanted me to know the answer. Below is that note in its entirety:

> When you asked me, what was the biggest change in me, I wasn't able to answer properly, because it was hard for me to bring back my thoughts. Before I started Nile, I was more selfish because that was what I learned in the public school. They taught us to be independent and reach our goals ourselves. However, at Nile they teach you how

to take someone with you and reach your goals together. I learned this from the teachers that gave hours in the school with the students and they showed me teaching is not only in the classroom. And how important it is to put others before yourself. After graduating from Nile, I had a better understanding what I wanted in life and what kind of person I wanted to become. So, I decided if I wanted to give back to the school, I had to follow in the footsteps of the teachers that gave to me.

Students

An 11th-grade female—born and raised in Astana, Kazakhstan—offered her perspective about such a course:

I love learning about other cultures. We're all humankind, but cultural maintenance is also important. I'm not against the new and innovations, but we can't forget our roots, our own heritage.

This young woman, whose immigrant Muslim families both worked, also spoke about how the school was preparing her for life. First quoting John F. Kennedy's famous line, "Ask not what your country can do for you, but what you can do for your country," she talked about what she wants to do for her adopted country:

I can do anything I want if I have knowledge. That's why this school is great. It gives me the knowledge to do it. I want to be an economist, learn how the system works. Then I can help other young people help the country prosper.

A 12th-grade Turkish Canadian, whose father was a photo journalist, had been at Nile Academy since the fourth grade. When asked why she and her parents chose and stayed here and not in a public school, her comments were remindful of student comments elsewhere:

The education is better. There is no bullying, drug use, or drinking like there, and you don't get to know one another or your teachers. Here, the teachers and administrators here are really friendly and help everyone more. The teachers and students come together and it's what makes us friends. I learned that not everything is done for money.

They love their job, do it for the sake of others and help others. I want to be one of these people.

Another child of Turkish immigrant parents, whose father was a real estate agent, was in the eleventh grade. She spoke also of a close relationship with teachers—their friendliness and helpfulness—as well as their conducting home visits. She talked about the students and teachers conducting a fundraising drive to help victims of the Nepal earthquake, which killed about 9,000 people (Rafferty 2020). The term respect came up, as it did in so many interviews everywhere, as she stated, "Everyone has respect for everyone, even the janitor."

A Somali senior, who said she "lost" herself in public schools playing hockey, found this school to have "less distractions" and her teachers to be "more caring." She explained, "They want the best for you. They want you to know that you're not making the journey alone."

Although this daughter of a taxi driver father and housewife mother had other positive things to say about her school, she also expressed a dislike for any religious component. When asked to explain, given no class in religion was taught, she said it was outside of school, primarily on weekends in the dormitory, about such things as saying the noon prayer (*namaz zohr*).

A senior, sent abroad to study by his Turkish parents (textile store owners), had attended Nile Academy all four years. With an acceptance offer from York University, he hoped to study there, and then become a computer programmer. In addition to playing football and basketball after school, he also served as a tutor to freshmen living in the dorms.

This place changed me and opened my view to the world. There will always be bad and good people, but we need to act differently. We should respect everyone, even when they are rude and mean. . . The people here are honest and always smiling. They are always helping. I too want to be part of this, not as a teacher but to help and share.

A Lebanese freshman, whose parents migrated in 1989, was the youngest of five children. His father didn't like the public schools, thought them dangerous and of low quality, so he insisted his son come to this school. The young man didn't want to come because "there were no girls." He complained about the small size of the gym and the lack of sports. Even so, he said his teachers were "very helpful," pointing to their comments on essays and do-over opportunities to improve upon them and thus learn from their constructive criticism. He hoped for a career in law enforcement.

A second freshman, the son of a Turkish accountant, was not looking forward to his sophomore year here. "If I could, I would start ninth grade over again someplace else." He too was unhappy in a boys-only school. He did like wrestling though, and that his teachers were "more tolerant."

> I will say they have helped me become more responsible, more independent, more serious about my future, and the person I want to become.

A third Turkish freshman, a Canadian resident since the age of two and whose father owned a cleaning franchise, also complained about the size of the school. Fond of his science classes and playing basketball after school, he also felt positively about his teachers:

> The Turkish teachers know our problems better. We don't have to answer questions we don't want to. Most are really nice. They help us solve problems that we sometimes can't talk to our parents about.

Another ninth grader also griped about the gym size, limited sports, and small school size. As with his classmates, he liked best his teachers for their caring, helpfulness, and interactive teaching style. An additional element he mentioned was "our religion [Islam] lets us relate to our fellow students and our teachers."

Another disgruntled student, a sophomore with Lebanese-Iraqi parents, said he would leave if he could. His parents sent him here to be in a different environment than his older brother who "gave in to peer pressure with smoking pot, drinking, and partying." He thought teachers favored Turkish students, as well as the dorm students over the commuters. He liked his Canadian teachers best because "they understand what we think."

We also spoke to a Canadian-born senior who liked his school in all respects. His mother and father (whose occupation was building restoration), had migrated from Turkey, and he was one of four children, two of them in college and the youngest in the third grade. He expressed satisfaction with "the teaching of culture, ethics, and tradition." And, like so many other students, he admired his teachers:

> We have close relationships with our teachers. We can talk to them whenever we want, tell them our feelings. They help us with our grades and are like family. This is true of the other non-Turkish teachers too.

Parents

Unfortunately, our schedule was such that we were unable to speak to as many parents as we would have liked. A few of the teachers interviewed were also parents of children enrolled at Nile Academy. One non-teaching parent interviewed was the father of twin girls enrolled in the school. He was a 1993 college graduate from Turkey and part of the Hizmet movement. The publisher of a magazine for the Turkish community, he spoke to the school's mission beyond teaching content:

> We seek to promote peace all over the world. People in this mosaic must learn to live together in harmony. People don't really know each other and need to talk, get their cultures together.

In a follow-up question about how his school tries to do this, he elaborated:

> The school offers global ethic values. Students get things from Canadian culture, but every culture has good things. There are different ethnic communities here [in the school] that we get together. They've had friends to age 13, but they have to find a good friend in this school environment. It's a good environment that helps character development. The teachers work hard and advocate this. They do not do this for the money. They love the children and make home visits.

Financial Supporters

A real estate broker, who emigrated from Turkey ten years earlier, had four children, but none were currently enrolled here because of "transportation issues." Nonetheless, he provided financial support to the school, as did other benefactors he knew who were not of the Hizmet movement. He spoke about his and their motivation to give money towards the school's operations:

> We all believe in the preservation of our culture, not the religious part so much but that of Hizmet. Some or a few students resent pressure about religion.

Another Turkish businessman dealing in paper import-export, had been living in Canada since 2001, and he had four children enrolled in Nile Academy. His financial support consisted mostly of providing scholarships to foreign students. When he was 22 years old, he joined the movement:

> They like to help people without any expectations. There is no quid pro quo. They will bring peace to the world. I really believe that. So, I became involved. And we help others of different faiths, for example, just recently we all worked together to help the earthquake victims in Nepal.

United States

Situated to the north of Mexico and south of Canada, the United States is also a vast land stretched between two oceans. Inland from its coastal regions are low mountains in the east and higher mountains in the west, with an extensive plains area lying in the middle. It is the world's third largest country, after Russia and Canada. With dense forests in the extreme north and deserts in the southwest, it is about half the size of Russia or South America, and slightly larger than China. With abundant farmland and natural resources, it contains the world's largest coal reserves, about 27 percent (CIA World Factbook 2020).

Representative democracy has been the bedrock of the United States since its founding as an independent nation. Its Constitution, ratified by the thirteen states in 1789, is the oldest one in the world. Controversy surrounding the 2020 presidential election and societal divisions notwithstanding, the United States remains a model for the world in offering freedom and equal opportunity for all its citizens.

Though impacted by COVID-19 like everywhere else, the United States relies on a technologically powerful economy. It is second only to China in Gross Domestic Product (GDP). However, while China is the world's leader in agricultural and industrial output, the United States is now a post-industrial society (Bell 1974). Accounting for 80 percent of the U.S. GDP are service industries, even though the country produces the second-largest industrial output (CIA World Factbook 2020).

Most relevant to the theme of this book is that the United States has long been the world's largest recipient of immigrants from all over the world. In recent years it has been averaging more than one million immigrants annually (1,031,765 in 2019). Europe typically now accounts for about nine percent of all immigrants to the United States, with those from Canada, Mexico, and the Caribbean accounting for about 29 percent. Approximately 38 percent come from Asia (includes Middle Eastern countries), with about 14 percent from Central and South America, and the rest from Africa, Australia, and New Zealand (U.S. Department of Homeland Security 2020).

Societal Overview

Of the 328+ million people living in the United States, 76.3 percent are white and 13.4 percent are black. Within those racial categories, 18.5 percent are Hispanic (who can be of any race). Asians and Pacific Islanders account for 6.1 percent. American Indians 1.3 percent, and people of two or more races are 2.8 percent (U.S. Census Bureau 2020).

Predominantly a Christian nation with 43 percent identified as Protestant and 20 percent as Catholic, the United States has 26 percent nonreligious, and numerous minority faiths. Chief among these are Jews and Mormons each at two percent; Muslims, Buddhists, and Hindus each at one percent (Pew Research Center 2019b). In comparison to other developed countries, the United States remains "a robustly religious country and the most devout of all the rich Western democracies" (Pew Research Center 2020). To illustrate, more than half of American adults (55 percent) say they pray daily. That is far higher than Canada (25 percent), Australia (18 percent), Great Britain (6 percent), and the average European country, which is 22 percent (Pew Research Center 2020). More than half of all Americans (53 percent) say religion is "very important" in their lives, with another 24 percent saying it is "somewhat important." Although the percentage of those saying either it is "not too important" or "not important at all" has increased over past years to 22 percent (11 percent in each of these two categories), Americans' belief in God is nearly nine-in-ten (89 percent). The highest belief percentages are found among Christians and Muslims, and the lowest are among religiously unaffiliated people (Pew Research Center 2015).

Schools

Before embarking on any commentary about Hizmet education in the United States, we must make a highly important distinction between charter schools opened by Turkish-Americans associated with the Gülen movement and with private Hizmet schools. About 125 of these charter schools operate in about 25 states and, although praised highly by parents and many state leaders, some have come under attack by conservative critics who claim that these schools promote "Islamic fundamentalism" while supported by tax dollars (Saacks 2016). In its relentless efforts to close all Gülen-inspired schools worldwide, the Erdoğan government asked the U.S. Department of Education to cut off the schools' funding, but it refused to do so, citing a lack of evidence (Jacobs, et al. 2019). As of this writing, no charges have been substantiated, although the critical onslaught continues, especially on social media.

However, no schools in this study are charter schools (schools privately run but publicly funded). Like all other schools previously discussed in this volume, Pioneer Academy is a private enterprise and receives no public funding. Founded in 1999 in the city of Clifton, New Jersey, this school moved in 2013 to its present location, a 17.6-acre campus in Wayne Township. Recognized by the New Jersey Department of Education and with Middles States accreditation, Pioneer Academy now offers coed classes from pre-K (Montessori school) through twelfth grade, and has a current total of 333 enrolled students within one large building complex.

On its website, Pioneer Academy declares its mission statement, one that is similar to those found worldwide at other Hizmet schools:

> Pioneer Academy provides a well-rounded, character-building education through challenging interdisciplinary curricula, stimulating extra-curricular activities, and community involvement. We seek to instill a lifelong passion for learning a strong sense of moral responsibility and a welcoming of diversity (Pioneer Academy 2021).

One-in-seven are international students living in dorms on campus. At the time of our visit, almost all of these students were from Turkey, but now none are, given the political situation there. Instead, the 35 resident students in 2021 came from such diverse countries as Azerbaijan, China, Germany, Japan, South Korea, and Ukraine.

Of its 37 teachers, nineteen hold advanced degrees, and fourteen are inspired by the Hizmet movement. With a curriculum focus on science, mathematics, cultural studies and language, the school boasts a 100 percent acceptance rate for its graduates to four-year colleges, including many prestigious universities. Students average SAT scores in the mid-600s and their average combined scores in the 1250s are the highest among all schools, public or private, in Passaic County, where the school is situated. About two-thirds of its graduating classes earn full college scholarships.

The then-school principal, a man in his late 40s, became interested in the Hizmet movement while a Turkish immigrant living in Australia. Helping to found the first Hizmet school there, he migrated to the United States and became the leader at this New Jersey school. He spoke to some of the challenges faced by Pioneer educators:

> Our first task is to correct our image. Some parents at the beginning see a few teachers with headscarves, but soon they find out that we are not a religious school. Our school is nonsectarian. We have no religious instruction. We have open houses and social media for introducing ourselves. Another challenge is financial. Some parents cannot afford the tuition, and thus we have scholarships. Then too, some parents ask us to give their children more attention than they can give them at home, and expect behavioral changes overnight. We do encourage senior students to mentor younger ones as role models and friends.

When asked to compare his school with Hizmet schools in other countries, he said they were closely aligned in being inspired by Hizmet, but with two differences. Home visits were "a challenge because American families like to be private." Secondly, there was a greater emphasis on Turkish language-and-culture course:

> Here we include the Turkish language because it is necessary to cherish ethnic awareness. This will also help to make the Turkish

language an international means of economic and scientific communication.

Such classes may serve these purposes, especially for students of Turkish ancestry, but because they constitute just 40% of enrollment, world language classes in Arabic and Spanish are also available. School officials are also considering adding classes in Chinese and French.

Again, we must emphasize a distinction between U.S. charter schools run by Turkish Americans that receive public funding and the Hizmet-inspired private schools that do not. The former has drawn criticism for claims like inconsistent teaching quality and fears about their allegedly teaching Islamic "fundamentalism." Actually, numerous advocates—including former Secretaries of State James A. Baker III and Madeleine K. Albright—have praised the Gülen movement as an alternative to fundamentalism (Knowlton 2010:3). Even so, the subject of our research is not these charter schools, but rather the private schools, which are highly praised and admired for their excellence.

Teachers

As elsewhere, the teacher interviewees in Canada and the United States revealed similar viewpoints and usually saw themselves as "agents of change." As one Pioneer Academy teacher said, "In a Hizmet school we educate the whole student—heart and mind." Similarly, another teacher—in a separate interview—offered this comment: "In Hizmet schools we do not focus exclusively on goals, rating and statistical outcomes. We do not overlook the most important consideration: the student."

That conveyance of education apparently works both ways. Another teacher was one of several to say something similar to her colleagues: "I treat teaching as more or less an honor, for I learned many things from it I might otherwise not have known about humanness." Another teacher put it this way: "It gives me great satisfaction in making my students feel worthwhile and in giving them the confidence they need to succeed, both academically and socially."

Perhaps that growth and satisfaction at least partly stem from the feedback that the teachers get about their work. Each morning before classes begin, the teaching staff meets to share and discuss their successes, failures, and challenges. All become aware of the larger scope of what is happening, and what steps might be taken to help or improve upon any situation.

Of course, with all its Advanced Placement and numerous other courses preparing students for college, the school's strong reputation rests heavily on its curriculum as well as its education of the whole person. For example, bridging both roles as teacher and parent, a middle school female teacher liked the rigor of the curriculum from primary grades through high school but, as a parent with children enrolled in the school, she also expressed strong appreciation for its character development:

> I am a parent, and I think the Hizmet School helps my kids to follow a straight path. For me the short-term gain is that my children learn moral values. Long term is that society is going to become a better society.

Students

A senior, who lived in Turkey until his father came to the United States three years earlier as a foreign exchange graduate student, lived in the Pioneer Academy dorms. In our conversation, he told us that his closest friends were all Turkish, that he found them more mature. Conversely, he felt closer to his American teachers because "Turkish teachers are more formal and harsher in their grading." Still, what he liked most about the school were his teachers: "They work with us. It is easy to talk to them." He also felt good about the school "promoting good values, good morals, good character." Playing soccer after school and enjoying trips to the malls, he liked his writing and forensic science classes, but lamented about "the lack of tutors here unlike the European Turkish schools. After graduating, he planned to take summer classes at Hofstra University, then go to New York University to major in international relations.

An Egyptian male student expressed satisfaction over his learning experience, but also recognized his personal development as well:

> Accepting others and showing tolerance are the most important values I have learned from my Turkish teachers and my non-Muslim classmates. I think this experience made me become more an open-minded person.

In other interviews of non-Muslim students, we heard similar re-marks and that this school "had changed [their] lives for the better."

Another Muslim student was a precocious 15-year-old who took Ad-vanced Placement courses and would graduate at the end of the academic year. With the ambitious goal of becoming a neurosurgeon, he appreciated the school promoting humanitarian efforts, and he had taken trips to Haiti and the Philippines to do such work. His father, who owned a taxi compa-ny, was from Dubai, and his stay-home mother was from Bangladesh. This commuting student told of difficulty in adjusting to school life:

> I was a minority and I did not know Turkish to talk to the other dorm
> students. I was able to bond much more easily with the Americans. My
> brother [who graduated this school four years earlier] told me not to
> give in. Once I learned the Turkish language, it was okay.

He also talked about the dormitory gatherings he experienced, where many subjects, including religion, were discussed. Although he was not a fan of these activities, he did appreciate the school promoting respect for one's elders and the "Hizmet campaign" to promote "human-ist acceptance of everyone." However, he was not fully enamored with his school:

> This is a good school but not the best. A few teachers take time with
> you and stay late to help, but just the Turkish teachers do this. Also,
> this place is too limited in athletics. I like wrestling, but to do that I
> have to travel 40 minutes away.

An 18-year-old dorm student from Turkey was excited to come to a school where there was a supportive community of Turkish fellow stu-dents. He said he looked forward to continuing support from the teachers and staff as well in "getting [him] through the next three years at Pioneer Academy." Another Turkish exchange student said, "I feel at home here. The teachers, the counselors, and even the principal are always willing to help." In a similar vein, an American-born Turkish male liked both the Turkish courses and student population: "My school environment encourages me to hold on to my identity."

Another exchange student made comments remindful of remarks by parents and students in other countries about Hizmet schools provid-ing a safe environment against bullying.

During my first year at boarding school in another place, I was bullied by students in my dorm. It was a hellish experience, made worse by the indifference of the faculty and administration, none of whom believed that it was their responsibility to see to my emotional well-being. The worst offender was my house master, who did nothing to encourage a sense of community in the dorm. Here it is totally the opposite. I am happy here.

An American-born Turkish student made an interesting observation that suggested his gaining knowledge beyond the subject matter:

I learned that high IQ does not imply wisdom. I learned what can go wrong when everyone tells you how brilliant you are, and you believe them. And, I learned that the smartest guy in the room can be wrong.

Another Muslim commuting senior came to the United States from Turkey when he was six years old. Of Bosnian and Kazakhstani heritage, he had been in Hizmet schools since the third grade because his father, active in the Hizmet organization, "wanted me to have exposure to others." He liked the school's emphasis on college because "it really motivates you," and he took eight Advanced Placement tests for college. He hoped to attend the University of Pennsylvania or Harvard to major in business or law. Despite his praise for the school's academic quality, he offered criticism about its shortcomings:

I don't like the small infrastructure or limited extra-curricular activities…. This school makes you less rebellious, and in a bad way it makes you less outgoing. This school is okay if you are an extrovert, but not if you are an introvert. American society is outgoing and diverse, unlike this school. I am very familiar with Hizmet because of my father, and this school does not practice Hizmet.

Pressed to explain his last point, his comments—now somewhat dated given the school's more diverse enrollment—included mention of the limited intercultural interactions, the overemphasis on Turkish and Islamic culture, and the narrower bonding between students and teachers. For someone living in the United States since age six, he appeared more keenly aware of the distinctions between a Hizmet school in the United States and one in other countries, a topic we shall soon discuss more fully.

Despite an occasional negative expression here and there (to be discussed more fully in the Retrospect section), most student responses were comparable to those in other countries we studied. A clear pattern of highly favorable attitudes about the school environment evolved, and for the same reasons that students gave elsewhere. They spoke about the teachers' high expectations, their "passion for their jobs" that "make us believe in ourselves and do our best," their "sacrifice of personal time to help us solve our problems, and their "encouraging us to improve ourselves."

Also dominating the responses of many students when asked what, besides their teachers, that they liked most about their school, was a class trip they took to another country. Time and again they considered it to be the highlight of their high school years. Their remarks suggested the trips were more than tourist-style sightseeing "in a bubble," but rather an intercultural experience. A Turkish young girl, for instance, declared, "I love trips to Haiti because I learn about Haitian culture." A non-Turkish male student reported, "The trip to Turkey helped to understand why my Turkish teachers are so different." [Sadly, trips to Turkey have been suspended due to political conditions there.]

Parents

In interviews with several dozen parents, we heard frequent praise for the administrators and teachers going out of their way to instill a strong work ethic in every student. For the many, this parent's comments serve to illustrate.

> Pioneer Academy teaches students to become self-motivated, responsible, and caring for those around them. It allows students to express themselves and develop teamwork, leadership skills and fair decision-making. I also very much like the Pioneer Academy because it offers a wide range of college prep courses designed to meet the needs of each and every student. Every student receives personalized academic, career and college counseling.

Little gestures or actions often can generate an attitudinal perception in the mind of someone who witnesses them. For example, one Christian parent found reassurance that way:

These teachers are practicing Muslims, but they follow a more moderate version of Islamic observance. I personally observed that the male teacher responds in a reciprocal manner when an American woman greets him with a handshake. *[Muslim men normally do not shake non-family women's hands.]*

Another non-Muslim parent had to be convinced to send her son to Pioneer:

We had resisted until a colleague of mine suggested that I visit Pioneer. At the end of my initial visit to Pioneer, it became very clear to me that this was the school I wanted for my son. Pioneer had a different atmosphere about it. All of attending students spoke very highly of the school. Students described devoted teachers and a rigorous academic program. Now that my son attends Pioneer, I can attest that Pioneer is the best that academia has to offer.

A Turkish parent liked both the academic and extra-curricular activities:

This school is excellent, and my son is very happy here. The school is challenging and the after-school programs are fulfilling. He has science Olympiad and soccer. He has never been happier in a school. This was his first year and, as the year comes to an end, he is already thinking about the next school year. The school is more than just a school It is like a family. They keep students in class for more hours, they set high standards for students and try to instill confidence in them.

Many parents, like this one, recognized that the school was doing more than providing a quality education with caring teachers: "They are guiding children to gain the self-control, self-motivation, and sense of responsibility they will need to hit their marks" In a separate interview, another parent stated, "They not only challenge students intellectually, but they also teach them to stand up for what is right." A third parent observed, "These teachers teach moral values, and encourage compassionate engagement."

Just as the students loved their intercultural experiences, especially on class trips to other countries, so too did the parents acclaim these practices. Said one parent, "The many cultural events and trips will help our children to appreciate cultural differences." Another opined, "We as parents are delighted that our children are exposed to different cultures."

Typical parental approval of the school's quality in all aspects is found in this mother's remarks:

> The teachers are very committed to their students and the curriculum is very challenging. The facilities and labs are top notch. Although Pioneer is a small school compared to others, it offers courses that none of the other schools do. It is an exceptional college preparatory school.

Financial Supporters

Pioneer Academy typifies other U.S. educational institutions in its fund-raising efforts. It too reaches out to alumni, parents, and friends for donations and scholarship funding. Several events are held each year to generate money for scholarships, class materials, and extra-curricular activities. In addition to these gifts and tuition income, the school—like all other Hizmet schools—partially depends on support from Turk-ish-born businessmen. In conversations with several of these men, we heard comments similar to those made elsewhere, most commonly their investing in the future to make the world a better place in terms of peace and harmony. One businessman also spoke about encouraging cultural maintenance, mentioned earlier in the parental comments:

> In this country where immigrants blend into the society, it is easy to lose your identity, to forget your roots, your culture, the values of your people. We must make certain our children never forget their heritage, their language, their beliefs, their customs, even their music and dances.

That concern is a common one among many immigrant parents. Throughout years of teaching courses on immigration and invitations to numerous ethnic events and talk shows, this author has often heard expressions of similar unease. Whether it is Japanese Saturday schools for the children of businessmen on temporary assignment in the United States, or Armenians and Greeks here who also run special cultural classes for their youth, or other organized efforts, the desire to hold onto one's uniqueness in a secular, pluralistic society is quite normal. The difference, perhaps, is that instead of a weekly activity, the effort is felt a bit more markedly in this school setting. An important portion of donations to school is coming from people with Turkish background. These donations, obviously, go a long way to enhancing the school's operations.

Retrospect

As expected, both similarities and dissimilarities manifested themselves in the Canadian and U.S. schools when compared to other schools included in this study. As elsewhere, facilities were modern with state-of-the art equipment. Emphasis on a STEM curriculum was evident as were the interactive teaching methodologies employed. Nevertheless, these private schools compete with larger public high schools typically located in affluent suburban areas. A few students, with such nearby contrasts, felt some relative deprivation in the range of sports and other activities available to them.

On a more positive note, students often spoke of close relationships with their teachers and praised their helpfulness. Tempered somewhat by the nature of the student population, the teachers' backgrounds, and the societal macro-culture, these comments, though certainly laudable, were not as effusive as we found in other countries. This pattern may have more to do with cultural influences than anything else.

The missions of these schools (providing quality education, instilling ethical values, and promoting intercultural understanding and acceptance) may be the same in Canadian and U.S. schools as elsewhere, but here the schools also have a fourth mission: cultural maintenance. Parents see in these schools a place where their children can preserve their Islamic identity in a secular, pluralistic society, so they won't feel stigmatized for being Muslims, and instead feel confident about their faith.

What, then, makes the Canadian and U.S. Hizmet schools unlike those in other countries studied, is the greater emphasis for Muslim kids on Islamic values and practices, as well as on Turkish culture for Turkish kids. Home visits may not be welcome in the United States or practical in Canada, but Turkish language classes, the food served in school cafeterias, and the informal gatherings at teatime are a few examples of how cultural identity and culture are strengthened.

Another distinction is found in parental attitudes. Everywhere, parents chose Hizmet schools for a quality education in a safe environment and, everywhere, we found many students continuing their education at universities. However, Canadian and U.S. parents far more strongly emphasized the college preparatory nature of the schools. Even though high-quality public schools were nearby, they saw the private schools as the better choice because of more highly dedicated teachers, smaller class sizes, and modern facilities.

As was pointed out earlier, there have been two broad reactions to Hizmet-inspired high schools in the United States. First there is skepticism and even criticism. The second is praise and admiration. In the next chapter, we will discuss these distinctions and others that we found among the Hizmet schools in the seven countries included in our study.

A Personal Note

The following commentary draws from Vince Parrillo's experiences as a visiting professor three times in Europe, lecturing throughout the continent at many other universities over several decades, and observing classes abroad taught by European colleagues. To him, some culturally different patterning in Western teaching styles, in comparison to European styles, became evident.

A cautionary note: the next set of remarks will be generalized comments, not universal truths, as individual teachers run their classrooms partly based on their personalities, age, and past educational experience. That said, American/Canadian teachers tend to be more informal with their students and European teachers are more likely to be formal, have a greater tendency to lecture more, and are less likely to encourage interaction in the classroom. Certainly, from the Canadian-born and American-born students we interviewed in those respective countries, we frequently heard that distinction made between Turkish and American teachers. The shared cultural identity between Turkish students and teachers perhaps increased the bond between them, as we heard often in these two countries, more frequently in Canada. All students praised their teachers' dedication and helpfulness, but seldom did we hear terms like "family" or "brothers" mentioned in the United States. This is a phenomenon we will discuss more fully in the next chapter.

References

Bell, Daniel. 1974. *The Coming of the Post-Industrial Society*. New York: Harper Colophon Books.

"Canada." 2020. *CIA World Factbook*. Retrieved March 1, 2021 (https://www.cia.gov/library/publications/the-world-factbook/geos/ca.html).

Gülen, M. Fethullah. 2004. *Pearls of Wisdom*. Clifton, NJ: Tughra Books.

Jacobs, Jennifer, Saleha Mohsin, and Nick Wadhams. 2019. "Trump Explored Cutting Grants for Schools Tied to Erdogan Foe." *Bloomberg News* (October 28). Retrieved March 1, 2021 (https://www.bloomberg.com).

Knowlton, Brian. 2010. "A Turkish Preacher Attracts a Following, and Incites Critics." *The International Herald Tribune* (June 12), p.3.

Oberheu, Caroline. 2018. "Major Religions of Canada." Society. Retrieved March 1, 2021 (https://www.worldatlas.com/articles/religious-composition-of-canada.html).

Nelson, Charles. 2005. "Fethullah Gülen: A Vision of Transcendent Education," Retrieved March 1, 2021 (http://citeseerx.ist.psu.edu/viewdoc/download?doi=10.1.1.506.8605&rep=rep1&type=pdf).

Pew Research Center 2015. "U.S. Public Becoming Less Religious." Retrieved March 1, 2021 (https://www.pewforum.org/2015/11/03/us-public-becoming-less-religious/).

Pew Research Center. 2019a. "5 Facts About Religion in Canada." Retrieved December 102020 (https://www.pewresearch.org/fact-tank/2019/07/01/5-facts-about-religion-in-canada/).

Pew Research Center. 2019b. "Trends in Religious Composition of U.S. Adults." Retrieved March 1, 2021 (https://www.pewforum.org/wp-content/uploads/sites/7/2019/10/Detailed-Tables-v1-FOR-WEB.pdf).

Pew Research Center. 2020. "Americans Are Far More Religious Than Adults in Other Wealthy Nations." Retrieved March 1, 2021 (https://www.pewresearch. org/fact-tank/2018/07/31/americans-are-far-more-religious-than-adults-in-other-wealthy-nations/).

Pioneer Academy. 2020. "Mission." Retrieved March 1, 2021 (http://pioneeracademy.org/index.php/school-profile/).

Rafferty, John P. 2020. "Nepal Earthquake of 2015." Retrieved March 1, 2021 (https://www.britannica.com/topic/Nepal-earthquake-of-2015).

Saacks, Bradley. 2016. "U.S. Schools Caught in Turkey's Crackdown After Attempted Coup." *Bloomberg News* (September 2). Retrieved March 1, 2021 (https://www.bloomberg.com).

Sawe, Benjamin Elisha. 2019. "Major Ethnic Groups of Canada." Society. Retrieved March 1, 2021 (https://www.worldatlas.com/articles/ethnic-groups-and-nationalities-of-canada.html).

"United States." *2020 CIA World Factbook*. Retrieved March 1, 2021 (https://www.cia.gov/library/publications/the-world-factbook/geos/us.html).

U.S. Census Bureau. 2020. "National Population by Characteristics: 2010-2019; Sex, Race and Hispanic Origin." Retrieved March 1, 2021 (https://www.census.gov/data/tables/time-series/demo/popest/2010s-national-detail.html#par_textimage_1537638156).

U.S. Department of Homeland Security. 2020. *Yearbook of Immigration Statistics 2019*. Retrieved March 1, 2021 (https://www.dhs.gov/immigration-statistics/yearbook/2019/table2).

8

THE GOLDEN GENERATION

This chapter primarily explores reflections and experiences of college students at Bedër University (see Chapter 3 about this university). All had graduated after completing at least eight years in Hizmet-inspired schools in Germany or Turkey, or in Madrasas (Islamic schools) in Albania. This material comprises from a follow-up study to those reported in previous chapters. It took place during Maboud Ansari's Fulbright assignment at Bedër University in Tirana, Albania in 2015.

Among the 30 student respondents between 20-22 years of age, were five males and 25 females, most of the latter intending to become certified teachers. All had chosen to attend Bedër University because they believed that, as graduates, they could attain rewarding careers in the global network of Hizmet schools. As in our previously reported studies, the majority of the respondents were from urban, middle and upper-middle class families. Almost all were Albanians, along with three German-Turks. All were Muslims, comprising 28 Sunni Muslims and two Bektashi Muslims. Their fields of study included Islamic Science, English Language, Philosophy, Turkish Language and Literature. In addition, some high school teachers from a Hizmet-inspired school in Pristina, Kosovo, were also interviewed.

As elsewhere, these one-on-one, semi-structured interviews, which typically lasted 1.5 to 2 hours, followed our university's research guidelines that ensured anonymity and privacy. Interviewees were freely selected through convenience sampling, without any input from college administrators. Questions mainly focused on the students' reflections and experiences while they were in high school, their plans, and what was their understanding and commitment to the educational philosophy of the Hizmet movement. More specifically, we sought to examine the effectiveness of their Hizmet-inspired education.

Theoretical Framework

Ibn Khaldun's concept of *asabiyyah* (solidarity), Karl Mannheim's concept of *generation*, and Ferdinand Tönnies' concept of *gesellschaft* provide a useful theoretical framework to gain a deeper sociological understanding of the Hizmet community, the social significance of Hizmet-inspired education, and its outcomes as regards the rise of what Gülen called the "Golden Generation." By that term he envisioned many of our social problems solved by a new generation infused with virtues to help the world, that is, by individuals who continually strive to become *insan-i kamil*, a perfected human being.

Ibn Khaldun (1332-1406) was an Islamic scholar, a social scientist, philosopher and historian, often described as the founder of the modern disciplines of historiography, economics, and sociology (often referred to as the "father of sociology." He was concerned with discovering and explaining the basic laws and principles upon which society operates. He described *asabiyyah* as the bond of cohesion among humans in a group-forming community. The bond exists at any level of civilization, from nomadic societies to states and empires (Ibn Khaldun 2015; Simon 2002).

Sociologist Karl Mannheim (1893-1947) was a seminal figure in the study of generations. In his 1923 essay, "The Problem of Generations," he formulated his theory. In this systematic treatment of generations as a sociological phenomenon, Mannheim posited that generations are only produced by specific historical events that cause young people to perceive the world differently than their elders (Mannheim 1998). Those who share a unique social and biographical experience of an important historical moment thus become part of a "generation as an actuality."

Mannheim's theory of generations is essentially a theory of social change (Laufer and Bengtson 1974). Indeed, his theory must be seen as one element of his broader interest in the sociology of knowledge. For Mannheim, the sociology of knowledge is the theory of the social or existential conditioning of knowledge by location in a socio-historical structure. Mannheim identifies generational location as a key aspect of the existential determination of knowledge. Generational location points to certain definite modes of behavior, feeling and thought.

German sociologist Ferdinand Tönnies (1855-1936) conceptualized ideal types that he called *gemeinschaft* and *gesellschaft* (*cemaat* and *cemiyet* respectively in Turkish), which are generally translated as "community and society" (Adair-Toteff 1996). His distinction between communal society and associational society helps us to understand the nature of social relations within the Hizmet community.

No such pure social type exists in the real world, only varying degrees of strength. However, as an associational *cemaat* society, the element of communal interest in the Hizmet community is stronger than traditional ties. It is held together by deliberately formulated prescriptions that are explained in terms of social-contract theory. Rules, norms and principles are rationally constructed in the interest of the larger entity that crosses religion and nationality. A bond of *asabiyyah* (solidarity) exists among individuals who are united around a common goal. It is this unifying principle that defines the Hizmet community. However, in practice the Hizmet community, like all other communal associations, manifests both kinds of wills (natural and rational) because human social conduct is neither wholly instinctive nor wholly rational (Wirth, 1926).

These three concepts as analytical tools can contribute to a deeper understanding of Gülen's "Golden Generation" (Yildirim 2004), and thus help us understand the process of becoming a member of the Hizmet community.

Schools

When asked why they chose Bedër University (site of all these interviews), this comment typified the heavy majority of responses: "It is an exceptional environment where I felt comfortable to pursue my intended career as a teacher."

Turkish-German students most commonly reported that they had chosen Bedër because they wanted to be part of a "diverse student body." Another said:

Here in this university, I have come to know many diverse groups of students. I respect the diversity of Muslims and appreciate their various cultural influences. My non-Muslim friends often do not know that Muslims are not a monolithic religious group. It is up to us to educate friends that Islam is not a monolithic group."

An Albanian student said, "My university has a very strong school of Islamic science, and I wanted to study under the best faculty in the country." *[As reported in Chapter 3, Bedër University has a Department of Islamic Studies, but also has six other academic departments.]*

When asked about their past schooling, respondents offered comments paralleling those reported in earlier chapters. All these college students reaffirmed that the Hizmet schools were well-known for their academic excellence and prepared them well for academic success. As one student said, "If it was not for the high academic standard, my parents would not have chosen this school for me." A young Turkish-German woman talked about her friend from Afghanistan who earned the top score nationwide on a college entrance exam and attributed her success to the education she received at a Hizmet school.

Another college student summarized Hizmet education in three words: "academic success, service, tolerance." All respondents reported that the quality of education provided by Hizmet schools is relatively high, especially in the field of physical sciences. In describing why they chose Hizmet schools, most reported four reasons: academic attainment, altruistic teachers, moral values and the chance to build relationships with both students and teachers. A German-Turkish student said, "I liked the school because it was a safe haven and the teachers played as role models for us."

As consistently reported in previous chapters, these respondents also affirmed that their Hizmet-inspired schools not only promoted pluralism and religious harmony, but also were free of prejudicial treatment toward or against any segment of the diverse student and faculty population. Further, all attested to the absence of explicit Islamic content in the curriculum and teaching. Instead, a general consensus emerged that those who were interested in religious issues could freely discuss them outside the class. One student passionately complained "Hizmet-inspired schools are generally misperceived as Islamic schools." Almost everyone shared the idea that their school had the same curriculum like other schools, but their school provided more laboratories and computer rooms.

A Hizmet school graduate from Azerbaijan now living in Germany, said, "No one gave me the *Quran* or pushed me to read the *Quran*." Respondents revealed close, emotional bonds with their high schools and strongly believed that Hizmet schools everywhere could contribute to the integration of Islam and modernity. One of the Turkish students spoke of his Iraqi Shia classmate in this way:

> Ali came to our school believing that we are Sunni and hostile to him. On our graduation day he told me that he never felt a minority or even away from home. I think my friend's story is a reflection of the Hizmet-inspired mission which is humanistic and non-religious.

The respondents also showed great appreciation for Gülen's philosophy of education. For example, one of the respondents who was nearing graduation said:

> When I was in my senior year of high school, a teacher told me to start to read philosophy because philosophy teaches you to think. Also, I think my reading of Gülen helped me to learn a distinctive way of being Albanian Muslim. I and my friends identify ourselves as moderate, or modern Muslims.

Students unanimously thought that their experiences that were either in Hizmet-inspired schools or in madrasas in Albania had changed their lives for the better. All called their schooling life-changing experiences that helped them "see the larger picture." The consensus was that their schools outperformed the public schools and they were grateful for their "excellent education." They revealed close, emotional bonds with their high schools and, as they prepared to "pick up the mantle," they had successfully integrated their faith and a modern perspective on life.

One participant, a visiting student from Frankfurt University, spoke of the popularity of Hizmet schools in Berlin and that "in my Hizmet school, values were taught through example, not through lecturing." A female student offered another point: "Educators in the Hizmet schools see teaching as a sacred responsibility and are aiming to bring about a marriage of mind and heart."

Teachers

As elsewhere, Hizmet-inspired teachers viewed their role as extending beyond the traditional educational one. For example, a teacher in the Hizmet-inspired school in Pristina, said,

> I have been actively involved in the Hizmet movement since 2014. I love teaching and I love to be around the students. In the Hizmet-inspired schools we are contributing to the larger community inspired by the idea "Golden Generation" by educating and training the younger members. I see my students as future members of this humanitarian movement. To me, the Hizmet schools develop and strengthen students' knowledge and have respect for freedom and human rights, including equality.

Another teacher at the same high school commented:

> Even though I had many opportunities and chances of getting better positions elsewhere, I preferred to be part of the movement and to teach here. After a year of teaching, I am glad to be part of the Hizmet movement. It is not so much religion itself that is influential, but rather the ways in which it has been interpreted and practiced that is influential.

Further insight into the heart of the movement came from this teacher:

> We are able to see the larger picture. The Hizmet movement functions as a force for social mobility. It offers students the opportunity to move up the socioeconomic ladder. If we look at the larger picture, we find the Gülen movement restored the humane face of Islam in the public arena.

The term *worldly asceticism* was coined by Max Weber in a study of Calvinist capitalism, but is equally pertinent to understanding Gülen's teachings in its perception of a daily activity in one's calling as a form of worship. The catalyst of his Golden Generation is educators, and so teacher training is essential to Gülen's vision. These teachers read Gülen's works independently, and subsequently decided to serve humanity through teaching. There is no formal institution to train these teachers other than the informal organization of "light-houses," or shared flats in which students hold weekly seminars and study meetings mostly during their college years (Michel 2003). Among the interviewed teachers from Gülen-inspired schools, we observed that most of them share certain characteristics in line with Gülen's teachings.

On the tradition of teachers visiting homes and the tea-time session, which we discussed in earlier chapters, one teacher spoke about the effectiveness of those visits: "I think in each of my home visits I obtained important information about family structure and the student. I know for fact that those students were encouraged and their performance improved."

In recalling those home visits, students often called them "beneficial" in improving behavior and instilling greater responsibility. "I think the home visit by one of the teachers was the most effective way to help me in my schooling," said one. Another who was studying to become a teacher said:

> Home visits are a sign of teachers' dedication and personal effort. The impact of home visits on my parents and me was great. Home visits by teachers and some school's principals are crucial to building an effective school environment.

Students

Before proceeding to the college students' comments, some important points should be noted. First, from the onset it was quite obvious that they were both open and excited to be interviewed. Moreover, almost all of them were well-versed in Gülen's writings, especially with regard to the topics of knowledge, science, altruism, humility, cultural sensitivity, activism, work ethic and self-criticism.

Nationalism

In recent years, many social observers have noted a rise in Albanian nationalism and ethnic assertiveness (Biberaj 2019). That pattern of ethnic pride clearly revealed itself among all respondents who identified themselves as Albanian, spoke of their rich cultural heritage, their pluralism, and long-standing religious harmony, as typified by this comment: "Pope

Francis, on his visit *[September 21, 2014]* to Albania held up Albania as a model of religious harmony. I am proud that Albanian interfaith harmony represents a unique example for the rest of the world."

Student comments clearly revealed a strong sense of Albanian pride existed at the forefront of their collective consciousness. They also exhibited an historical awareness of the sufferings of their parents and grandparents, who suffered significant personal and economic losses during the 50 years of Communist dictatorship. Their family histories affected their worldview as revealed in comments such as this student's observation:

> Those of us who have come to understand Gülen's philosophy have gained different perspectives about our existential identity. We Muslims here emphasize also our Islamic identity as an element in defining our Albanianness.

Understanding Gülen

Interviewees continually referred to Gülen as a scholar, imam, and teacher. One student said, "Our generation does not idolize Mr. Gülen, but we know him as one of the most influential preachers of Islam today." That influence was evident in all respondents saying they followed Gülen's principles. No doubt some of that influence comes from informal conversations with teachers, as indicated by this student's comment:

> My teacher respects him as a charismatic leader, and I see him as a Muslim reformist who promotes a version of Islam that embraces the sciences, education and interfaith dialogue.

In fact, respondents who were familiar with Gülen's writings saw themselves not as followers but as sympathizers. They also rejected claims that the Gülen Movement is a religious cult and Fethullah Gülen is a cult leader.

One of the respondents who seemed to be well-versed in Gülen's writing spoke of his worldview:

> There are three major enemies of not only Muslims but also humanity as a whole: ignorance, poverty and disunity. Actually, the Hizmet educational project that I did go through covered all these three areas.

With regard to the importance and distinctiveness of the teachings of Gülen, many reported that they were part of a new generation of activists "who are altruistic and cherish diversity and pluralism." A German-Turkish respondent reported that "Hizmet learning convinced me to understand that Turkish Islamic heritage is capable of adjusting to modern times."

These college students exhibited a broad intellectual perspective that allowed them to see clearly the separation of state and religion, such as: "Mr. Gülen thinks the perceived conflict between religious knowledge and science is falsely conceived." Another referenced one of Mr. Gülen's famous statements that Islam and democracy are compatible. "Some ignorant people in the media label the Gülen movement negatively. To me and my classmates, it is about democracy and Islam."

Improving Society

Native Albanian students talked with great intensity about major social problems in their country. Longstanding issues of blood feuds, dependency of many families on the money coming from relatives abroad (13% of the GDP), justice reform, and the high unemployment rate of educated Albanians all re-emerged in every interview.

Regarding the relevance of their Hizmet-inspired high school education, respondents frequently expressed the belief that the Hizmet schools help advance democracy through knowledge, universal values, and discipline. A 22-year-old Albanian male spoke of writing an article about how young Albanians can work for democratic reforms. In his essay he was critical of "frozen democracy," or elite-dominated democracy. He also expressed appreciation for the teachers who helped and encouraged him to do a presentation at a national conference.

Students also had a list of complaints and demands for change, such as correcting the achievement gap in their country's schools. One participant said, "Current inequality among high schools is not acceptable. Changes are needed to make the high school admission process more accessible to low-income families." A similar criticism had to do with the uniqueness of "elite schools" in the Hizmet network. For example, a student who had already obtained a teaching certificate said, "In our country *[Albania]*, public education should function as an equalizer."

Her main point was that the Hizmet schools should create fairer access for highly qualified low-income families. The problem, however, is these schools have limited capacity and not all low-income student, even those who score well on placement tests, can be accepted.

Although many students expressed a desire to improve their society, they essentially wanted to do so through the means of promoting open, reciprocal relationships, rather than political action. They characteristically understood the Gülen movement to be a social and educational one. Still, they acknowledged the Hizmet network, as a transnational and significant community, naturally might have political influence.

Intercultural Events

With regard to intercultural events that are standard at all Hizmet-inspired schools, one student disclosed how such trips broaden perspectives:

> It was not until our field trip to Haiti, where my idea of poverty and those affected by it was influenced. Before the trip, I did not understand the complexity of what it meant to be poor. I had grown up in a middle-class family with financial security but in my high school times, when I became aware that not every family is like ours, one of my teachers encouraged me to become friends with one of my classmates who was challenged with the issues of poverty.
>
> I think it was the teachings of Mr. Gülen that changed my perspective and helped me feel empathy. In many ways the field trips opened my eyes to the challenges poor people face when living in poverty. Teachers encouraged our class to make donations for a family that was facing the challenge of poverty. After my high school graduation, I became involved in humanitarian aid.

Like lower-grade students everywhere whom we had questioned, these college students highly valued their field trips and travel abroad during the school year. Almost every participant talked about positive experiences resulting in personal growth and empathy:

> Because of the field trips not only did we learn more about ourselves, but we also met new people and learned new ideas. I was fascinated by the diverse cultural heritages of Muslims. I returned home with a new perspective on cultural differences and their impact on Islam.

Such extra-curricular activities are a significant feature of the Hizmet schools. Looking back, these alumni now saw such activities as contributions to the larger society and as an important way for individuals to serve their community and country. It would seem that the normative power of the Hizmet-inspired movement helped shape this younger generation of high school graduates. They often mentioned that their involvement in these activities helped them to become a better person and serve something greater than oneself. Another common remark about their extracurricular activities was that they encouraged student bonding and made them appreciate intercultural relationships.

Becoming Part of the Golden Generation

Students often used the expression "my generation" in their comments. This self-identification is an indication of the social significance of age (within historical time) in the development of the Hizmet community. What became evident is that the Hizmet education model has produced a common generational consciousness which constitutes the essential social capital for social change. From a sociological perspective, it is this distinctive historical consciousness that characterizes the "Golden Generation."

This generation, evidenced through all these interviews, has a strong sense of *asabiyyah* (social cohesion) and a unique generational consciousness. Born within the same historical and cultural context, they have been exposed to similar experiences during their formative youthful years that have shaped their attitudes and future plans.

These Hizmet graduates have been educated and influenced in a way that makes them willing to embark on a lifetime journey of "service" (Hizmet), and they are prepared to serve their community and country. They believe that they have been called upon to bring about social and cultural change. They are, as Fethullah Gülen envisaged, agents of change as "ideal persons," ones who are well-educated, particularly in natural sciences and foreign languages (Gülen 2004). As he hoped, they plan to use their knowledge and training for the service of humankind. To illustrate:

> I am among the rising educated of potential migrants in this country," said one teacher education student. "If I get a teaching position in the Hizmet schools abroad, then I, as a younger follower of Hizmet, would serve my country as well as the community I live in.

One participant, a graduate from a high school in Germany, specifically identified herself as part of Gülen's Golden Generation and considered him "one of the most influential scholars of Islam today."

> My generation is mostly self-taught by the Gülen Movement's website. Our thoughts, actions, and inspiration are influenced by Mr. Gülen's ideas. Mr. Gülen always encourages everyone, including the Turkish entrepreneurs, to support quality education. In our informal gatherings when we talk about social problems, we often make references to Gülen's writings and sermons on the Internet.

Another student viewed entering the teaching profession as a means to create a better world for Muslims:

> The main sources of structural problems in Muslim societies are ignorance and poverty. By becoming a teacher, you can make a difference.

An Albanian student envisioned becoming a teacher as a way to help Muslim youths to transition into contributing, moderate members of society:

> Youths in Albania have been exposed to the media's presentation of the violent spread of the political Islamists. However, through education we can answer youth's ambivalent questions of identity, politics and faith.

Similarly, a German-Turkish student commented:

> As we know there is a rise of Islamophobia in the West. We as teachers will be capable of explaining the harsh challenges of being a young Muslim in the West.

Another Albanian student regarded teaching not merely as a job, rather than a calling to improve society:

> As modern Muslims, we could contribute to the advancement of a more prosperous and more pluralistic Albania.

These future teachers also exhibited a deep appreciation for the importance of early education in shaping middle-of-the-road attitudes and values. A typical comment was:

Early life exposure to moderate forms of Islam is an effective way against the danger of extremist recruitment.

These interviews exemplified Gülen's success in having people inspired by his ideas produce his "Golden Generation." Time and again came student testimony that their educational career choice, heavily intermingled with altruistic goals, drew inspiration from older role models. Almost all the students praised their teachers' devotion, altruism and knowledge. The following comments are but one example:

> I'd like to teach as an English teacher in the same high school where I studied. During my high school years, I came to know so many teachers. Their unselfishness, sympathy, and their love for teaching caught my attention and I want to become a teacher like them.

Although these students came from both Hizmet-inspired secular schools as well as the religious madrasas, there were striking similarities in their experiences. All respondents, regardless of which school they attended, had been actively engaged in at least three Hizmet school projects. Most of the respondents believed the extra activities improved their social skills and helped them become more self-confident.

Financial Supporters

Although he did not interview any financial supporters during his Fulbright stay, Prof. Ansari learned that his respondents were fully aware of the link between the Gülen movement and Turkish business people. One respondent mentioned her paper, "Turkish Businessmen in Emerging Markets in Central Asia." In her paper, she wrote that Turkish business people are willing to support Hizmet initiatives because of its "emphasis on hard work and education as a solution to poverty."

Another student, who was German-Turkish, stated that her father, a businessman in Turkey, joined the movement when he learned that Mr. Gülen urged his followers to "build schools instead of mosques." She added that "my parents believe that the schools are far more important to shape moral character."

A third student, with parents who operated a medium-sized company, noted, "The business model of the Hizmet movement reflects Gülen's values and sponsors' activities in a pluralistic way."

Retrospect

It was apparent from the first interview to the last that, unlike most respondents previously discussed, these college students were well-versed in Gülen's writings and in the media's coverage of the movement, particularly regarding the Hizmet-inspired schools.

A significant similarity between these Hizmet high-school graduates was that—although diverse in nationality, locale and type of past schooling—all commended the effectiveness of their schools' methods of teaching. They all described their experiences at their Hizmet-inspired schools as rewarding and life-changing. Like the repeated comments of middle and high school student reported in earlier chapters, these alumni of Hizmet-inspired schools were full of admiration for their high schools' quality of education. In general, the respondents also revealed their awareness that the education system in which they were involved was built on Hizmet core concepts, and they were grateful for the high quality of education that they received.

That said, many differences nevertheless usually exist in the attitudes, values, behaviors, and lifestyles found within a generation as there are between generations. However, the presence of *asabiyyah* (solidarity) prevailing through shared commitment to Hizmet principles, enables the Golden Generation to function collectively as active agents as well as in their own individual capacity.

The Hizmet community of *gesellschaft* is an outcome of rational will in modern society despite the *gemeinschaft* presence of religion. But as we have come to understand the Hizmet community, the element of communal interest is stronger than traditional ties. The community is held together by deliberately formulated prescriptions that can be explained in terms of social-contract theory. In the Hizmet community, rules and principles are rationally constructed in the interest of the larger entity that crosses religion and nationality. It is this bond of unity or *asabiyyah* among individuals which defines the Hizmet community.

However, in practice, the Hizmet community, like all other communal associations, manifest both kinds of wills (natural and rational). As we know, human social conduct is neither wholly instinctive nor wholly rational.

Also, the theory of generation contributes further to our understanding of the concept of the "Golden Generation" conceived by Fethullah Gülen. It helps explain the process of becoming part of the newer generations within the Hizmet movement.

Combined, these three concepts help to explain the rise and expansion of the Golden Generation within the socio-historical location of the Hizmet movement.

Perhaps a note of caution should be made here. As a limited qualitative study, this small sample mostly included college students who identified themselves as high school activists during the open-ended questions. Therefore, their reflections and responses may not represent the complete picture of the Hizmet movement. We will have more to say about the Hizmet-inspired schools in the next, concluding chapter.

References

Adair-Toteff, Christopher. 1996. "Ferdinand Tönnies: Utopian Visionary." *Sociological Theory* 13:58-69.

Biberaj, Elez. 2019. *Albania in Transition: The Rock Road to Democracy.* New York: Routledge.

Cahnman, Werner, ed. 1973. *Ferdinand Tönnies: A New Evaluation.* London: Brill.

El-Banna, Sanaa. 2013. *Resource Mobilization in Gülen-inspired Hizmet: A New Type of Social Movement.* New York: Blue Dome Press.

Gülen, Fethullah. 2010. *Toward a Global Civilization of Love and Tolerance,* Clifton, NJ: Tughra Books.

Ibn Khaldun, Abû. 2015. *The Muqaddimah: An Introduction to History.* Princeton, NJ: Princeton University Press.

Mannheim, Karl. 1998. *Essays on the Sociology of Knowledge.* New York: Routledge.

Michel, Thomas. 2003. "Fethullah Gulen as an Educator." Pp. 69-84 in *Turkish Islam and the Secular State: The Gulen Movement,* edited by Hakan Yavuz and John L. Esposito. Syracuse, NY: Syracuse University Press.

Park, Bill. 2008. "The Fethullah Gülen Movement." *Middle East Review of International Affairs* 12:1-14.

Simon, H. 2002. *Ibn khaldun's Science of Human Culture*. India: Syracuse University Press.

Yavuz, M. Hakan. 2013. *Toward an Islamic Enlightenment: The Gülen Movement*. New York: Oxford University Press.

———. 2003. *Islamic Political Identity in Turkey*. New York: Oxford University Press.

Weber, Max. 1958. *The Protestant and the Spirit of Capitalism*, translated by Talcott Parsons. New York: Scribner.

Wirth, Louis. 1926. "The Sociology of Ferdinand Tönnies." *American Journal of Sociology* 32: 412-422.

9

Comparisons and Conclusions

This field research occurred over a four-year period, beginning in 2012 in Albania, then Bosnia and Herzegovina. Kazakhstan was the locale in 2013, followed in 2014 by Romania and Poland. In 2015, Canada and the United States were the final countries included in this study, while Albania became the locale a second time for a 2015 follow-up study with Hizmet school alumni.

Our selection of these countries enabled cross-cultural comparisons of western and nonwestern countries, of Muslim-majority and Muslim-minority countries, and of fairly homogeneous and pluralistic countries. Admittedly, much has changed since 2015, most obviously the Turkish government targeting anyone and anything even suspected of a connection with the Hizmet movement, as well as COVID-19 disrupting life everywhere, including school attendance. Still, the information gathered presents many insights into the educational practices in Hizmet schools outside of Turkey.

One primary and two secondary research objectives guided this multi-year study. Regardless of country, the Gülen-inspired schools seek to promote moral values and acceptance of all peoples while emphasizing math, science, and technology in their curriculum. How well the schools succeed in achieving these three goals in different cultural settings was our primary focus. Also, with critics claiming that the schools have either a political or religious hidden agenda, we sought to determine if either assertion had merit.

By interviewing the educators, students, parents, and financial supporters in each country, their multiple viewpoints—no doubt af-

fected by the cultural milieu and national history of each country—
provided a good variety of input. Those responses and positive comments, admittedly, went far beyond our expectations as they provided
a treasure trove of information and insight into how the functioning of
Hizmet-inspired schools affected the mission of this educational model.
As expected, some differences existed in country-by-country comparisons, but far more similarities revealed themselves. This chapter dis-
cusses both.

As mentioned in Chapter 1, our investigation operated from a sociological perspective. As academic outsiders, we sought information
from insiders either within the movement or from non-members with
direct involvement in the schools, either as students, parents, or employed teachers. The sociological lens shaping our review was the theoretical framework of negotiated order theory involving structure and
process (Strauss 1978). Our cross-cultural comparison study was an effort to determine how a changing cultural milieu would affect Hizmet
school goals (conveying modern knowledge and promoting ethical values). How mitigating were these external social forces upon the reason-
ably uniform structure shared by these Gülen-inspired schools in alter-
ing processes in different countries? What changes, if any, occurred in
curriculum, interactions, or pedagogy? Were there different patterns of
instruction or participation?

What follows is an attempt to answer these questions, within our
theoretical framework, about cultural differences impacting the Hizmet
schools, their success in achieving their goals, and if there was any hidden political or religious agenda.

Structure

What makes these schools so popular, as our interviews revealed, is that
they are very well regarded for their high standards of scholastic achievement, especially in areas unaccustomed to experiencing excellence in
education. Furthermore, they are remarkable in the Muslim world in
their commitment to secular modern learning that is open to students
of all backgrounds, male or female (Barton 2007:657). Early childhood
classes naturally take place in a neighborhood school, but through a
written-exam competition, geographically dispersed, high-achieving

older students—whether rural or urban, poor or affluent—can earn full or partial scholarships to live in dorms and get that private-school education.

If one universal truth exists about these schools, regardless of their location, it is that they provide a high-quality education through a rigorous curriculum, and that was a prime factor in parents selecting such a school for their children. Everywhere we went, parents expressed great satisfaction about small class sizes and the level of education provided, saying it gave their children excellent preparation for college and careers. Many were unaware of the underpinnings of the Hizmet movement, only that the "Turkish schools" were better, in their minds, than others.

Some schools were sex segregated, while others were coeducational. However, one characteristic permeated all of them: Female students were equally encouraged to participate in all science, math, technology courses and academic competitions. Among female educators we found one commonality typically existing among those in western cultures: They were intelligent, articulate, and possessed a good self-esteem. However, in the schools we visited, no woman was the head administrator or second in command. Some women were part of the administrative leadership, usually in such areas as admissions, counseling, foreign student facilitator, or psychologist, but not otherwise.

Upper-level leadership, both in foundation membership and senior school administrative positions, is Turkish. In their early years of operation, most of the teachers are also Turkish. They are either transfers from an established school somewhere, or recent college graduates, often products themselves of a Hizmet elementary and/or secondary school, who—as many stated to us—"want to give back" and "give others the same educational experience they had." As the schools become more fully established, the faculty and support staff usually become mostly native residents.

Within modern facilities that we found in each country, the educators benefit from smart classrooms (high-end digital technology, including interactive whiteboards, display capabilities from online sources, academic software, and well-equipped laboratories). Just as all these buildings and equipment are comparable in their state-of-the-art quality, so too is the curriculum similar from one place to another. Of course, some variations in subjects do occur, as required by each nation's accreditation standards. However, a consistency exists in an educational program with most courses taught in English, with an emphasis on math, science, and technology.

Through our general observations, and confirmed by responses from all participants, Muslims and non-Muslims alike, the Gülen educational model is not only modern in pedagogy and content, but also is essentially secular. A course in religion is not part of the rigorous curriculum, although some schools did offer a comparative religion class or an ethics class. None was theological though. Nor could we find testimony about any direct or indirect attempts at political persuasion, although we gently queried students. None could recall any of their teachers making such attempts. However, several students in Albania did speak to a hope for elimination of widespread corruption, which is a well-recognized reality (see *CIA World Factbook* 2020). And, in Bosnia and Herzegovina, some Bosniak students complained about the political divisions in their country (its tripartite leadership) and that Serbians wouldn't carry the Bosnian flag. It appeared, though, that these political observations resulted from external factors unique in those two countries rather than internal influence from within the school.

This educational model, in its structure, is thus based on educators' understanding and interpretation of Gülen's philosophy of education. However, there is more to the model than the inclusion of western scientific thinking, and an emphasis on the English and Turkish languages. Gülen's humanitarian ideas are also an essential component of the model, and they manifest themselves in the educational process. It is through the actual practices occurring in the schools where the complete model finds realization, even if slightly modified by different cultures.

As previously mentioned, except for the madrasas, there is an absence of explicit Islamic content in Hizmet-inspired schools' curriculum; religion is *not* taught in these schools. In fact, many Muslim parents told us they believed that teaching religious values is the responsibility of parents, not the school. Moreover, students consistently reported the lack of any pressure, neither to conform or convert to Islamic practices in any way. Instead, the international and interreligious mixture in other schools sets the tone for an ecumenical teaching environment.

...[T]he schools are as at least as secular in their teaching program and formal orientation as contemporary mainstream denomination Christian schools. In this respect they are very much like modern Anglican, Presbyterian, Methodist or Catholic schools and as such don't have the overtly religious character of many independent Christian or Jewish schools (Barton 2007:657).

Regardless of their faith, parents admired their school's efforts to instill ethical scruples. They frequently praised the fact that the curriculum promoted universal values, diversity, multiculturalism and reflected the compatibility of Islam with pluralism, secularism and democracy. Terms we frequently heard, like "better person," "heart and mind," and the "whole person" were indicative of something occurring beyond the transmission of content knowledge and skill development. Although inspired by Islamic values, Hizmet educators are actually practicing a secular form of "lifestyle evangelism" (Bornstein 2003; Aldrich 2006). Such character-based education, with its focus on character strength, is one that parents interviewed readily accepted.

Many Hizmet schools in different countries are decidedly elite in two ways. First, their excellent reputations create a heavy demand for entry in Asia and Europe. As reported in previous chapters, successful finalists in the competitive entrance exams represent only a small fraction of those seeking acceptance. The result is a student body of the more gifted and talented. Second, scholarships may mitigate the financial challenge faced by some families to meet tuition costs, but the reality is that the majority of families usually come from a higher socioeconomic status. The majority of parents had a college education, and they were professionals from the upper middle class in such fields as business, diplomacy, education, engineering, law, and medicine. We certainly spoke to students and parents from working-class backgrounds, but far more often they were from the upper-middle-class. One other dimension of the student population was that their ethno-religious diversity reflected the general characteristic of the region in which they lived.

We found an internal consistency between Gülen's philosophy of education and practice in the Hizmet-inspired schools that we visited. That philosophy appeared to play an important role in the success, expansion and popularity of these schools in all countries. The similarity of the participant responses indicated that there was one model evident in all Hizmet school education. Moreover, their responses reaffirmed that this universally applied educational model played a key role in students' academic, social and emotional development. Thus, we conclude that the performance of these Hizmet-inspired schools is consistent with their stated mission.

Process

Implementation of any educational model is the key to its effectiveness and practicality. One consistent finding in our interviews with teachers in all seven countries was their belief in serving as role models to provide a character-based education. A second regular component of the learning dynamic—again frequently brought forth in interviews with students and parents—was recognition of the efforts by teachers to develop close, friendly, helpful relationships with their students. These schools may be furnished with expensive technological equipment and founded with noble intent, but the everyday interactions of educators and students are the real determinants of effective learning.

When structured transmission of knowledge within a formal classroom occurs through an intimate teacher-student relationship, the learning experience is far more productive. New buildings and the latest technology are fine, but successful education relies not just on teaching competency, but equally importantly on how well these professionals care for those in their charge. In essence, teachers' attitudes determine the effectiveness and lasting impact of any educational efforts. To borrow a line from James Russell Lowell, it is "not what we give, but what we share, for the gift without the giver is bare" (Lowell 1848/2016).

Lowell's poem, "The Vision of Sir Launfal," is about the brotherhood of man and altruistic charity, two elements found in great abundance among Gülen-inspired educators, as our interviews revealed. Independently of one another, and from one country to the next, they frequently expressed their belief that the most effective giving is in caring about, and providing, for their students' full potential, whether in knowledge, skills, or character development. Many spoke of teaching as a "moral calling," one through which their own behavior serves as equally important companions to the formal classroom instruction. Like teachers everywhere, they derive meaning and significance from their work, but additionally see themselves as building a better world as role models for others to become "better persons."

Teachers revealed shared ideas and commitments expressed in the form of secular humanitarianism, not in any religious dogma per se. They saw themselves as "agents of change," that they each could make a difference. Echoing thoughts about inner change from as disparate sources as Mahatma Gandhi and Michael Jackson (see the lyrics of "The Man in the Mirror"), these educators strive to be the change they want in the world through their own attitudes and actions. All teachers believe that they are helping to build the next generation, but Hizmet teachers envision their effort as more than developing civic competence and critical thinking skills. They see themselves on a mission to inculcate lasting ethical values, to champion compassionate engagement. They freely give their time and energy to their students without expecting material gain in return. Through their sense of responsibility and altruism, they consider hard work and self-sacrifice to be important attributes, ones they hope to pass on to their students.

For these teachers, teaching is a mission and they were willing to adapt themselves to very different environments. Almost all male educators had six or more years of similar work experiences in African and Central Asian countries. With rare exceptions, female educators were native to the country in which they worked. Regardless of gender, all gave indications of their commitment to a view that they were on a journey together to build a better world through the next generation. They displayed a shared group identity, holding deep communal feelings that formed a powerful bond. Dedicated teachers, with high expectations for their students, both in their scholastic achievements and in serving all humankind, determine what happens in these schools.

As authors, we are but two of the hundreds of thousands of educators who found role models in one's own teachers and drew inspiration from them to choose the same career. The same can be said of many clergy of all faiths who were similarly influenced through personal contact with other members of the cloth. Not surprisingly then, we encountered university students, often the first in their families to attend college, who said they wanted to "give back" and become Hizmet teachers. They extolled their former instructors as great teachers and role models who gave them an "enriching experience," one they wanted to offer to others. So many said that the experience prepared them for success and made them more receptive to unlike others by fostering open-mindedness. Their apparent commitment to serve in the Hizmet movement illustrates that, as these schools prepare students for successful lives, they also serve as a farm system, like professional baseball, to strengthen the movement with fresh, young talent. Not all teachers of Hizmet schools are products of this system but, indeed, many are.

The Role of Culture

Although the Gülen educational model possesses a transnational consistency in structure and goals, it is culturally responsive, even in a non-Islamic milieu. In each country the schools meet national standards, follow the state-mandated curriculum, and consequently possess official accreditation. Although most classes are taught in English, others are taught in the native language, most commonly grammar and history classes. Solid academic content, mixed with a nurturing of moral development and humanitarian values, are school hallmarks in all cultures.

Before addressing variances in cultural influences upon the schools, some commentary on the pervasiveness of Turkish culture in these schools should be stated. This presence and that of Turkish educators are why they were known as "Turkish schools." Regardless of the schools' locale, Turkish language and culture are an obvious element of these schools. The name *Gülen* and the term *Hizmet* were unknown to most parents we interviewed. Instead, parents—most especially Christian parents in Poland and Romania—strongly supported multicultural events, many of them mentioning the importance of trips to Turkey, and they spoke favorably about the exposure of their children to Turkish culture. Sentiment abounded among these non-Muslim parents that multicultural events would likely facilitate intercultural understanding in the next generation. In one form or another, many expressed a view that such commonly held values as tolerance and acceptance transcended cultural differentiation. '

One component of Turkish culture promoted in the schools are language courses. These are optional, but they are highly popular elective choices among students. Other cultural facets to be found in most

schools are Turkish foods served daily in the cafeteria, activities in cele-
bration of holidays, and school-sponsored class trips to Turkey.

Another element of Turkish culture is teatime, a pastime also popular in Bosnia and Kazakhstan. Sipping tea from a small, tulip-shaped
glass is so ingrained into Turkish culture that virtually no business
transaction, conference, meal, or social meeting can take place without
several glasses of *çay*. Often at these schools, "teatime" occurred after
regular classes end, and this cultural tradition serve a dual purpose of
informal social interaction and moral guidance. In this setting teachers, students, and university students serving as tutors shared tea and
conversations on topics not explicitly taught, such as cultural norms
and values, or such personal characteristics as time management, responsibility, punctuality, kindness and self-confidence. During their
interviews, students often commented favorably on these sessions,
sometimes even without being asked. As one Bosniak male student
said, "We like teatime because we learn a lot about moral and social
values. We learn from each other and from our teachers." A Kazakh
boy commented, "At teatime we talk about how the most important
thing is who you are and how you behave with others; it's not money."
In contrast, where teatime is not part of the culture—Poland, Romania,
Canada, and the United States—this practice was not as integral a part
of Hizmet school culture.

Elements of Turkish culture thus become disseminated rather
ubiquitously among those of other ethnic backgrounds. Non-Turkish
and/or non-Muslim students frequently spoke about their receptivity
to such intercultural interactions. In schools with enrolled international
students, that positive responsiveness extended was even broader. Importantly, this cultural diffusion also impacted on the Turkish students as
well. With the noteworthy exceptions of Canadian and U.S. schools—to
be discussed shortly—Turkish students also divulged a greater understanding and appreciation for other cultures. Collectively, student comments affirmed that they were not only comfortable in their diverse environment but desired to make the most of it.

Such attitudes are hardly surprising, given the intent of Hizmet educators to build bridges between people of different faiths and national
backgrounds. Consequently, faculty and staff do not simply rely on inci-
dental interplays among students from diverse cultures to develop an un-

derstanding, appreciation, and acceptance of people unlike themselves. In bonding with their students through outside classroom activities, by setting an example through their words and actions, and by organizing cooperative in-or-out-of-class activities (e.g., group projects, anti-poverty undertakings, fundraising efforts for disaster relief), these educators seek to instill altruist attitudes and values.

Cultural Mitigation

Aside from adapting to curriculum requirements of individual countries (including specific academic units in language, math, science, history, health and physical education), the schools embodied at least one prevailing sentiment within the host country. In Albania where widespread corruption is well known, those interviewed often spoke about honesty and trust as the main social problem to be overcome. Respondents in Bosnia and Herzegovina, whose family histories held painful memories of death and destruction in the mid-1990s, the elimination of interethnic conflict through the schools' mission of brotherhood would help, they believed, their society to heal. In the Central Asian country of Kazakhstan, quality schools whose curriculum furthered the restoration of Kazakh culture, language, and history, after decades of Russian suppression, was a key factor in natives' desire to assert their ethnic identity. In Poland and Romania, each fairly homogeneous in Christian religions, a shared predilection among respondents appeared to be an emphasis on experiencing diversity. Canadian and U.S. schools, on the other hand, drew greatest support for their preservation of Turkish and/or Muslim attributes in the context of an overwhelmingly diverse society.

Naturally, in Muslim-majority countries that was the prevalent religious composition of the student population, and vice versa in Muslim-minority countries. However, in middle schools, and even more so in secondary schools, ethnic diversity was significant, Kazakhstan was a bit less diverse than in other countries visited, but nonetheless existed also. That was far less the case in Canada and the United States when we called on these schools. These administrators admitted to difficulty in attracting non-Muslim families. Elsewhere, poor-quality public schools served as a push factor to drive parents to seek quality private schools, but here the nearby public schools, which were mostly suburban, were competitors. Furthermore, in these two immigrant-receiving countries, diversity was already the norm and less of an inducement.

Home visits, something often praised by students and parents in the Eastern Hemisphere countries we visited, are another important component of Hizmet school practices that create an interconnectedness among students and their families with the school. However, like teatime, this feature too is mitigated by culture. In Canada, as mentioned in the last chapter, even Turkish-Canadian parents prefer their privacy, and so home visits were not encouraged. Elsewhere, visitations are constrained because of the limited number of Turkish staff members. Therefore, the educational model is not always far-reaching into homes as elsewhere, and is constrained to what occurs within the school setting.

Without question, the macrocultures of Canada and the United States play a critical role in affecting the daily operations of Gülen-inspired schools compared to other countries included in this study. Elsewhere, the schools are secular and Turkish subjects are optional choices. Many of the elementary and secondary schools are international, with many non-Muslim families choosing to enroll their children because of the safe environment and quality education. In Canadian and U.S. schools, cultural diffusion is the norm, with the mostly non-Turkish students exposed not only to Turkish culture, but other faiths and/or nationalities as well. Conversely, Canadian and U.S. schools are more homogeneous with Muslim students, because they have difficulty recruiting others, as just mentioned. These schools primarily appeal to Turkish parents, desirous of cultural maintenance. International students are either from Turkey or are Muslims. Religion may not be taught in the school but, for dormitory students, we heard about weekend "religious conversations" from some, and these were not always welcomed.

In Albania, Bosnia-Herzegovina, Kazakhstan, Poland, and Romania, parents sought out the "Turkish schools," as they were commonly known, not only for safety and quality reasons, but also because they promoted multicultural education and interaction. In Canada and the United States, parents admired the strong college preparation teaching, but also found in the schools an ethnocentric oasis against the pluralistic surroundings where ethnic identity and values could be diminished by such outside social forces.

Even though the Canadian and U.S. private schools we visited serve as protective cultural shelters for Turkish Muslims, they do not shut out the outside world. After all, as repeatedly mentioned, one tenet of the Hizmet movement is promotion of intercultural understanding. So, for example, class trips to Haiti serve as one means to acquaint students with another culture, one that does not threaten to undermine the cultural maintenance function of the school, in comparison to the prevailing dominant culture. In addition, clothing drives or disaster-relief fundraising served as another means to promote intercultural cooperation in a safe manner while preserving Turkish culture in a pluralistic society promoting assimilation.

Some Caveats

Of course, no educational institution is perfect and Hizmet schools are no exception. Although the teachers interviewed were certainly impressive, and students praised them highly, a few did complain now and then about a particular teacher. How much of this was teenage griping because of a grade or some other factor, we could not detect. Perhaps such cultural norms like cultivating self-reliance and thus less top-down dependency, so prevalent in the United States and Canada, embolden students in those countries to criticize more freely.

Still, it is quite reasonable to consider that not every teacher possesses the personality and teaching skills to shine in the mind of every student. All of us can recall teachers who didn't hit the mark. And, despite the Gülen philosophy that modern science is one of the critical elements of education, one biology teacher—according to at least two of his students—penalized students for challenging their comments against the theory of evolution. Perhaps though, the exception does indeed prove the rule. As trained and experienced interviewers who listened to extensive testimony from students and parents, we can say with confidence that Hizmet teachers are seen as highly dedicated professionals whose formal and informal actions with their students create a highly positive and learning experience.

Several Muslim resident students did experience religious pressure from some residence hall assistants, particularly about *salah*, the daily prayers that constitute the second of five pillars in the Islamic faith.

It is possible the parents may have asked school officials to help them teach their children in dorms about certain essentials of religious practice. Although this is conjecture, we do know that we just heard such complaints only a handful of times in Muslim-majority schools here and abroad, even though we pursued that line of questioning among all resident students. Therefore, we believe such instances were exceptions, not a common practice. As previously mentioned, no religion class is taught in any school we visited, just courses in comparative religion or ethics. Based on the hundreds of interviews we conducted, ones where anonymity and confidentially were assured under the guidelines of our university's Institutional Review Board (IRB), and except for the few minor exceptions noted above, our research found no evidence of a religious agenda, a finding consistent with other research (Ebaugh 2010; Tittensor 2012).

Similarly, we found no evidence of a hidden political agenda either. Whether such an agenda existed in Turkey, as Erdoğan charges, was outside the scope of this study. We focused on Gülen-inspired schools in differing cultures outside of Turkey. Although Turkish cultural diffusion is occurring through optional courses, cultural events and trips to Turkey, we found no challenges or suggested alternatives to political authority, either directly or indirectly. And, it needs to be said, we tried to find any evidence of same.

Conclusion

The Hizmet movement, also known as the Gülen movement, is a collective initiative of a group of people who follow altruistic ideals that are rooted in Fethullah Gülen's new interpretation of Islam and the neo-Sufi tradition. What makes Gülen consequential is the existence of followers who are compassionate about his ideas and strive to put them into action. The movement inspires people across the globe, regardless of ethnicity, religion, and culture. The universal values it promotes such as tolerance, pluralism, scientific pursuit, interfaith dialogue, and the importance of democracy are the bond of *asabiyyah* (solidarity) among both activists and sympathizers. This well-organized community of people (not a political party) has the mission of serving humanity. Gülen advocates that transformational change can be achieved through what he calls a "Golden Generation" of young people who combine intellectual enlightenment with spirituality (Park 2008).

Our field research in seven countries found that the Hizmet-inspired schools in each of those different cultural settings have similar broad objectives. They were all modern institutions with secular education and high standards, and they have been successful in fulfilling the requirements of modern education. Within them exists the normative power of the Gülen movement to educate and shape the younger generation into Hizmet advocates and practitioners.

The manifest function of the Hizmet educational model, then, is to produce an excellent secular education, as well as promotion of shared universal values and cultural tolerance among a diverse body of students. Not only do the schools enjoy great reputations for their rigorous curriculum and high standards, but also this educational model cultivates bonds of caring between teachers and their students.

Moreover, the educators, students, and parents take great pride in their openness to diversity, and in an atmosphere that nurtures a strong sense of interconnectedness with others, regardless of their backgrounds. This broader notion of learning tends to bring together individuals who, outside this point of contact, would be less likely to become familiar with one another. Students develop positive expectations, attitudes, behaviors, and values that will shape their future adult lives.

No matter the country, no matter the ethnic make-up of the student and teacher population in each, the three main goals around which the Hizmet schools are structured—a quality education emphasizing STEM subjects, a solid grounding in ethical behavior, and inspiring intercultural harmony—were consistent in both effort and success. Cultural variations exist, to be sure, but they do not detract from the parallel processes that are occurring. What is happening in these schools is nothing short of admirable.

As this book goes to press, the demonization of the Gülen movement continues in Turkey and increasing numbers of suspected Gülen sympathizers are being purged in waves of arrests and many are still detained. The Turkish coup attempt was universally condemned and Fethullah Gülen was among the first to denounce it. However, Hizmet activities in Turkey are banned and the Gülen movement was formally declared a terrorist organization in May 2016.

Despite the widespread suppression in Turkey, Gülen movement activities, including about 1,000 Hizmet-inspired schools, continue to operate in 140 countries around the world. A great body of research, including ours, confirms the fact that the Gülen movement is a transnational community and its appealing mission for "the betterment of human life" has already had significant impact on the global order (El-Banna 2013).

Of great significance also is the fact that Gülen-inspired schools educate females and males equally, unlike most other types of Islamic schools. Indeed, in oft-repeated instances we heard girls and young women speak of gaining self-confidence, a trait readily observed in the interviews. In many parts of the world where traditional gender roles are still prevalent, the successful education of females in STEM subjects and in their social development is an impressive achievement.

The intercultural and influential Gülen movement has shown great potential for transformational change in education. Many social movements throughout history have dramatically changed the societies in which they occurred. With its remarkable success, the Gülen movement continues to be a major social and educational force in the world. As this study and many others have revealed, the Hizmet movement is no longer a community of Turkish diaspora but a "citizen's organization" across the globe.

Despite its demonization and treatment by the Turkish government as an oppositional political party, responses—both individually and collectively from within the Gülen movement—have typically been principled, nonviolent, and lawful actions. Given these external pressures and internal reactions, the Gülen movement has now entered a new lifecycle. This new phase may necessitate those in the Movement to re-examine its organizational and strategic features. Like any other social movement that faces obstacles, including the loss of resources, the Gülen movement must be prepared for trends that may play out in the future.

From a sociological perspective, there are always clear causes why some social movements decline while others succeed. Successful social movements are those that constantly readjust to the changing circumstances. The future of the Gülen movement remains to be determined, but its promotion of ethical values, humanitarian concerns, and interfaith dialogue should resonate across generations.

References

Agai, Bekim. 2002. "Fethullah Gülen and His Movement's Islamic Ethic of Education." *Middle East Critique* 11(Spring): 27–47.

Aldrich, Joe. 2006. *Lifestyle Evangelism: Learning to Open Your Life to Those Around You.* Colorado Springs, CO: Multnomah Books.

Barton, Greg. 2007. "Preaching by Example and Learning for Life: Understanding the Gülen Hizmet in the Context of Religious Philanthropy and Civil Religion." Pp. 650-662 in *International Conference Proceedings: Muslim World in Transition: Contributions of The Gülen Movement.* Leeds, UK: Leeds Metropolitan University Press.

Bornstein, Erica. 2003. *The Spirit of Development: Protestant NGOs, Morality, and Economics in Zimbabwe.* Stanford, CA: Stanford University Press

Çetin, Muhammed. 2007. "The Gülen Movement: Its Nature and Identity." Pp. 377-390 in İhsan Yılmaz, ed. *Muslim World in Transition: Contributions of the Gülen Movement.* London: Leeds Metropolitan University Press.

CIA World Factbook. 2020. "Albania." Retrieved March 1, 2021 (https://www.cia.gov/library/publications/the-world-factbook/geos/ro.html).

Ebaugh, Helen R. 2010. *The Gülen Movement: A Sociological Analysis of Civic Movement Rooted in Modern Islam* (New York: Springer).

El-Banna, Sanaa. 2013. *Resource Mobilization in Gülen-inspired Hizmet-A New Type of Social Movement.* New York: Blue Dome Press.

Gülen, M. Fethullah. 2010. Toward a Global Civilization of Tolerance and Peace. Somerset, NJ: Tughra Books.

Koç, Doğan. 2016. "Strategic Defamation of Fethullah Gülen: English vs. Turkish." *European Journal of Economic and Political Studies* 4:189–244.

Lowell, James Russell. 2016. *The Vision of Sir Launfal and Other Poems by James Russell Lowell.* North Charleston, SC: CreateSpace Publishing. Originally published in 1848.

Strauss, Anselm. 1978. *Negotiations: Varieties, Contexts; Processes, and Social Order* (San Francisco: Jossey-Bass).

Tittensor, David. 2012. "The Gülen Movement and the Case of a Secret Agenda: Putting the Debate in Perspective." *Islam and Christian-Muslim Relations* 23:2 (March): 163-179.

Tittensor, David. 2014. *The House of Service: The Gülen Movement and Islam's Third Way.* New York: Oxford University Press.

Turam, Berna. 2007. *Between Islam and the State: The Politics of Engagement.* Stanford, CA: Stanford University Press.

Watmough, Simon P., and Ahmet Erdi Öztürk. 2018. "From 'Diaspora by Design' to Transnational Political Exile: The Gülen Movement in Transition." *Politics, Religion & Ideology* 19 (May): 33-52.

INDEX

A

Abrahamic Gatherings x
accreditation xii, 58, 85, 123, 155, 160
accredited 45, 58, 84, 102
Agai, Bekim 15, 17, 18, 22, 23, 26, 168
Albania 47-61
  alumni 55-56
  parents 56-58
  religious schools 49-50
  secular schools 50-51
  societal overview 47-48
  students 54-55
  teachers 52-54
American blacks xiii
architecture 41, 54, 59
asabiyyah 138, 139, 147, 150, 165
Azerbaijan 59, 124, 141

B

Bektashi Muslims 47, 137
Balkans 21, 46, 61
Bedër University 59, 60, 137, 139, 140
Bosna Sema 33, 34, 44
Bosnia and Herzegovina 31-46
  ethnic cleansing in 31
  financial supporters 44-45
  first Hizmet school in 33
  parents 42-44
  schools 33-34
  societal overview 32-33
  students 36-42
  teachers 34-36
  war in 34
Bosniaks 32, 34-36, 42-44, 156, 161
Bucharest 25, 79, 80, 85, 87, 90
bullying 41, 42, 82, 128
Burch University 33, 40, 44

C

Calvinist capitalism 142
Canada 111-121
  cultural comparisons 161-164
  financial supporters 120-121
  parents 120
  school comparisons 132-135
  societal overview 111-112
  students 117-120
  teachers 114-117
Catholic 32, 40, 41, 43, 48, 68, 78, 91, 92, 95-99, 104, 105, 107, 108, 112, 114, 122, 157
Çela, Alba 47, 60
cemaat 139
Central Asia 15, 21, 29
Çetin, Muhammed 15, 27, 168
charter schools x, 123, 125
Christians xiii, 81, 100-104, 123
co-educational 51, 59, 65
communist domination 77
conflict 17, 32, 54, 80, 83, 93, 145, 162
coup attempt ix, 16, 166. See also July 2016
Croatia 35, 91, 99

D

diaspora 167
diversity x, 19, 32, 36, 39, 41, 46, 52, 61, 69, 75, 89, 123, 140, 145, 157, 162, 163, 166
dormitory 33, 34, 51, 54, 73, 89, 103, 118, 127, 163

E

Ebaugh, Helen Rose xi, 15, 19, 22, 27, 165, 168